The
Patriarch

THE LIFE AND LEGACY OF
ZIADEH (JOHN) HANNA FARHAT

By Family and Friends

With Kenneth R. Overman

"Tell me about your husband."

"He's an honest, sincere, loving man. He love everybody … there was no hate in him. He is one-of-a-kind, and so very special."

"Go on."

"I miss him a lot. I would give up everything in the world and live in a tent just to have him back. That's what I am wishing."

Jeanette Farhat - November 2016

Table of Contents

Introduction

When Ziadeh (John) Hanna Farhat passed away on October 23, 2016, he left behind an extended and loving family whose desire it is to preserve his legacy for future generations. This book is only one of many ways his life will remain in the hearts of those who knew him. While this is not an extensive chronology, it does highlight his role as husband, father, grandfather, business and church leader, advisor, and faithful friend. Indeed, John lived an exemplary life from the time he set foot on American soil. But, the roots of his strong character and moral code go back to a Palestinian city named Ramallah.

The end of World War II brought many changes to Palestine. First, the United Nations mandate established the new State of Israel and in the ensuing chaos of redefined borders and resettlement, many residents of the prosperous city of Ramallah decided to leave. So in 1948 at the age of 14, John boarded a cargo ship in Haifa and sailed half way around the world to New York. From there he took a train to the city of Detroit where he landed his first job in a bowling alley. Then he worked in a production line at the Ford car factory. Seven years later, he went back to Ramallah, married his young bride, Jeanette, and returned to the U.S. to settle permanently in Jacksonville, Florida.

For the next 69 years, John worked tirelessly to raise his large family and build a thriving business. His home also became a refuge for newly arriving Ramallah immigrants. His life prospered, but not without challenges, including one tragic event that would shake the foundations of any man. But his roots in the Orthodox Christian Church were deep, and they played a crucial role in maintaining both his faith and his role as family patriarch.

The story of John Farhat is told through third person narration, interviews with family and friends, and several vignettes. Regardless of the source, every perspective in this book points to this: John was a deeply caring individual who lived for his family and others, instead of himself. Proof of this legacy is evident in his offspring, where values of integrity, faithfulness, and loyalty are often unspoken but evident through their daily life.

Another expression of John's love for family exists in his large, successful business on Normandy Boulevard called Green Acres Sporting Goods. The business grew from a small convenience store, to an enterprise with 20,000 square feet of everything a sportsman could want. Today, Green Acres is one of Northeast Florida's largest privately held sporting goods retailers catering to a sizable number of the population, including several of Jacksonville's elite.

While *The Patriarch* is written for his immediate family and friends, any interested reader of biography will gain deep insights into the success story of an immigrant, an entrepreneur who pursued the American dream. The message is clear, particularly in the current political climate when immigration—the lifeblood of our culture and economy—is in question. People like John Farhat arrive with a desire to build a new life, and their solid moral values and work ethic have always produced a net gain for all of us.

So now, read on to learn about the hard work, faith, family, and legacy exemplified by the Patriarch himself.

Downtown Ramallah – 1950s

Downtown Ramallah today

Prologue

A Wedding in Ramallah

"Ramallah" … composed of "Ram," meaning height and "Allah:"
the Arabic word for God

July 11, 1954

The crush of guests spilled from the ground-floor foyer and out to the courtyard. Some conversed in low voices while others looked with anticipation to the stairway where Jeanette, the bride to be, would make her grand entrance. According to plan, she would emerge from a second-floor bedroom followed by her mother and her aunt, and descend the wide, circular staircase to her waiting grandfather. He would then take her arm and escort her to the altar where her future husband stood.

Just inside the downstairs dining room and out of sight, a slim, handsome groom with receding black hair paced the floor. His dark, western-style suit with a white shirt and striped tie made him look thinner, even taller, than the average Palestinian. In the two weeks since he arrived from America he had experienced a flurry of activity, but finally Ziadeh (John) Hanna Farhat would be married.

John's wife-to-be, Jeanette, was a young teenager when his father pointed her out in the schoolyard. He saw her from a distance, leaning down playing a game of marbles with her girlfriends. At age fifteen she was about to be married, although she wasn't aware of it at the time. That wasn't unusual since all girls born in Ramallah during that period had pretty much the same story. Not only did they marry young, they had to marry within their own clan to ensure the money or property remained in the family.

"John was in America a long time," recalled Jeanette in 2016. "He had returned to Ramallah for a visit, and his mother brought him to the school to meet me. They stood outside until I walked out. That night, my cousin next door called the house and said they're going to come and see me. When they arrived, I was supposed to serve them coffee."

John saw Jeanette only three times before they were married. The first time was in the schoolyard. The second was right before his father—along with a dozen or so family members—went to the house of his bride-to-be to conduct the traditional *tulbeh*, when he asked Jeanette's grandfather (in the presence of the entire family) for her hand in marriage. Of course her grandfather said yes, because that was just a formality. John was not allowed at that meeting since his father, in the presence of the rest of his family, did the asking. That done, they all sat down for a pleasant time of drinks, food, and conversation. Jeanette served the coffee.

She laughed with the memory.

"I was so shy … I was so young at the time and I didn't know what was going on. John's father, grandfather, and uncles—decided to visit my parents that night. When they were there a while, his father asked for my hand in marriage to John. But I didn't know anything about it."

She shook her head.

"Then they told me I was engaged to this guy. I said, 'What? … I haven't even finished my high school.' But they said, 'No, you're going to be engaged instead.'"

The engagement ceremony took place at Jeanette's house. Again, everyone was present, but this time their local Orthodox priest played a role. He took Jeanette and her parents aside, and asked if she agreed to marry John. When everybody said 'yes,' more celebration followed, including a "betrothal ceremony" also conducted by the priest.

In former days in Ramallah during the engagement ceremony, the groom's father would present a purse filled with gold coins to the bride's father as a form of dowry. In this case, Jeanette's grandfather received the dowry since her father died at a very young age in Spain. But for John and Jeanette's wedding, a ceremonial passing of a purse with no gold inside sufficed; both families were fairly well off so a dowry was not necessary. With the wedding date set, the couple began to assemble their *trousseau*, or wedding clothes. John's wardrobe consisted of a suit and tie, and that was that. But Jeanette's clothing needs skyrocketed, so her entire family got in the act.

The third time John saw Jeanette happened the evening before the wedding, when he hastily gathered his clothes from his bedroom and passed her on his way out the door. That was the one night he was not allowed to sleep in his own bed. As tradition dictated, he stayed at the home of his best man. The following morning, John donned his new wedding clothes and, accompanied by at least a hundred of his clapping and singing acquaintances along the way, walked back to his father's house.

They say you can tell how well liked the groom is by how many people turn out to welcome him when he walks to the place of the wedding. It seemed that John Farhat was very popular because it looked like the whole town turned out: close relatives, distant relatives, friends, acquaintances, and a few complete strangers.

All that happened within two weeks of John's return. It had been a crush of activity, including high anxiety for his future role as husband and provider. Now as he paced the floor of the dining room he realized he might not even be over his jet lag. One of his uncles saw his apprehension and slapped him on the back.

"Do not worry … it will all be over soon and then you will have your bride!"

John was all of 20 years old. Although he trusted his parent's good wishes—as well as his own judgement of character and good looks—the arrangement to marry this girl caught him slightly off guard. He knew it would happen long before he arrived because he'd discussed it with his parents through letters and infrequent, expensive long distance phone calls. But it had been six years since he left home to work in Detroit. After a few odd jobs there, he landed a good position in the Ford factory assembly lines making more money than was ever possible in Ramallah. Only when he "made his bones," was he able to take on a wife. Now that he was back, he was anxious to get the ceremony over with and move on with their new life. He stopped pacing. Somehow he knew he'd made the right choice even if his parents thought it was all their idea.

Jeanette stood in stockinged feet vigorously fanning her face with a handkerchief while her mother and aunt mumbled and fussed over her wedding gown. She hoped to look poised and confident when she made her grand entrance: a tall order for a teenage girl who met her husband-to-be only two weeks before and would soon leave the only home she had ever known.

Fanning harder, she stood up straight to let her mother smooth the gown and adjust her veil. Moments later, the six-piece band on the veranda began to play. Stiffening with resolve, Jeanette started to walk toward the staircase.

"Your shoes!" her mother hissed. "Put your shoes on ... and your flowers!" Jeanette backed up and stepped into her high-heels, smoothed her dress again, accepted the small bouquet of flowers offered by her aunt, and walked to the top of the stairs.

It looked like all of Ramallah had gathered in and around the home of Hanna and Sarah Farhat—John's parents. But that was normal since weddings constituted one of the largest events in any Palestinian's life and everyone was expected to participate. Weddings were life after all, which meant the one-time celebration had to be a good one. Fortunately for Jeanette, her future in-laws were among the wealthiest families in Ramallah, and because the groom's parents paid for the wedding, this one would be over the top.

With her mother and her aunt close behind, the bride descended the stairs, one careful step after another. She was aware of the quiet that fell on the crowd as every eye turned to her. Finally she stepped onto the landing, and to the waiting arm of her grandfather. Then the crowd parted and they walked out to the veranda.

"The wedding was so beautiful," recounted Jeanette. "Everybody came. We walked about a half mile to the Greek Orthodox Church where we had the ceremony."

In those days the Greek Orthodox Church was the official church in Palestine. All Christians worshiped there until their own version of Orthodoxy found a home in their community. In the case of the Farhats, theirs was called Antiochian Orthodoxy.

"There was a lot of singing and dancing as each of our families celebrated, "she said. "When the ceremony was over, we walked back to his parent's house for the reception. That too was very beautiful. There were trees throughout the courtyard, with tables placed beneath their shade. And of course piles and piles of food waited for us."

"One of the first things I did," she continued, "was to step over a lamb that had been killed. It was a fresh one, and as tradition went if the bride steps over a fresh, uncooked lamb on her wedding day, she will bear many children. Well, my husband, John, had two sisters and no brothers, and his parents wanted more boys born into the family. So that's exactly what happened ... we had four sons and a daughter!"

One week after their wedding, John boarded another cargo ship in Haifa and sailed back to America to arrange for his new wife's visa. In so doing, he would be one of thousands who, after centuries of settlement in the Ramallah area, would reverse the trend of migration.

(L to R) Lamia, Sarah, Abla, and John at age four in Ramallah

Farhat house in Ramallah – built in the early 1900s

John, Jeanette, Sarah and Hanna Ziadeh Farhat – 1954

John and Jeanette Farhat – 1954

Chapter 1

Roots

Until 1948, the entire population of Ramallah descended from one man named Rashid Haddadeen who relocated from southern Jordan in 1562. He moved there for two reasons: first, there was a Greek Orthodox monastery there, and second, the area of Ramallah boasted lush, green forests. Since Rashid was a blacksmith (Haddadeen means "blacksmith") he had a plentiful supply of wood to fuel his trade. Rashid married, and soon the population grew from a settlement, to a village, and eventually to a city. Ultimately the entire population of Orthodox Christians descended from Rashid Haddadeen were all related to one another in some way.

Ramallah remained relatively peaceful and prosperous until 1907, when the first of three major waves of emigration began. In 1907, the city was still under the rule of the crumbling Ottoman Empire struggling from the effects of the costly Balkan Wars. To shore up their armies, the Ottomans began conscripting young Ramallah men, starting at age 12. Fearing the demise of their male youth, parents began to ship their sons to other parts of the world, primarily America. In 1922, Hanna Farhat—John's father—along with many others, sailed to New York and then took a train to Detroit. For the most part, the young men travelled alone. Considering the nature of close family relationships and their love of the land, such a transition was indescribably difficult. But in America there was security, money to be made, and greater opportunities.

Hanna started out as a door-to-door salesman offering household goods to employees of the many car manufacturers and steel mills around Detroit. His success eventually led him to make sales throughout all 48 states. When he earned enough money he would return to Ramallah for a short visit, and then return for more work. He never flew, preferring to take slow cargo ships between Haifa and New York (apparently his brother was killed in a plane crash early in his life, so he swore he'd never set foot on an airplane). But that wasn't so bad. Cargo ships of that era—known as tramp steamers—provided a selection of fairly nice cabins for paying passengers.

Hanna's trips to Ramallah continued after his arranged marriage to a pretty girl named Sarah. Of course, every time he returned to Ramallah, Sarah became pregnant. A year after his first trip home he met his first born, and then another child was conceived. After his third child was born however, Hanna couldn't see his family for twelve long years; the Second World War broke out and he couldn't leave America until it was all over. Meanwhile, Hanna became a full-fledged American Citizen. Fortunately, U.S. immigration policy at the time automatically allowed his children to become citizens even if they were born in Ramallah.

***

Starting at the end of World War II until 1948, the demographics of Ramallah changed from 100% Christian, to 75% Christian and 25% Muslim. That's when the second major wave of emigration began. It was a complicated period in Ramallah's history, so it will help the reader to know more about the events that shaped John's life.

Britain had ruled Palestine since the early 1900s, but by the end of the Second World War the weakened British Empire was unable to continue so they deferred the problem to the United Nations. In November of 1947, the UN passed the United Nations Partition Plan for Palestine. The proposal was largely influenced by the Zionist cause to establish a Jewish state, and with the eventual backing of the United States, it easily passed.

The UN partition divided Palestine into three areas: an Arab state, a Jewish state, and a "Special International Regime" for the cities of Jerusalem and Bethlehem. But the partition allocated more than half of Palestine to the Jews in spite of the fact that Jews made up less than half of Palestine's population. In response, the Palestinian Arabs—aided by volunteers from other countries—resisted the Zionist forces through protests, many of which resulted in violent skirmishes. Nevertheless, by May 14, 1948, the Jews had secured full control of their allocated share of Palestine, including significant parts of Arab territory.

On that same day in May—which marked the expiration of its mandate—Britain withdrew its army and the State of Israel was proclaimed. The very next day, forces from Egypt, Transjordan, Syria, Lebanon, and Iraq invaded Israel. That was the start of the ten-month long Arab-Israeli War. Although the shooting eventually stopped, years and years of heavy diplomatic maneuvering would follow. Among the many outcomes was 700,000 Palestinian Arabs either fled or were expelled from their homes in the areas that became Israel. Over the same period, around 700,000 Jews immigrated *to* Israel, many of whom were expelled from their previous countries of residence in the Middle East.

Until then, residents of Ramallah had free movement between the West Bank, Jordan, Lebanon, and Syria. However, the effects of the war followed by continuing tension throughout Palestine and Israel, with frequent incursions from both sides, naturally garnered a strong sense of unrest. It became apparent to those living in Ramallah (as in the rest of Palestine) that their good life had become a vanished dream. Once again, natives of Ramallah began to emigrate, primarily to the United States. In 1948, John followed the footsteps of his father, Hanna, and at the age of 14 he too sailed for America. Hanna, however, returned to Ramallah to watch over his wife, two daughters, and his ailing mother.

Not long after the Arab-Israeli War, the neighboring country of Jordan annexed a significant area of Palestine, including Ramallah. The political powers of the day named the annexed territory the "West Bank." That marked the beginning of the "Jordanian Era," the first of an intended peaceful expansion by Jordan throughout the region. It lasted until July 20, 1951, when an assassin killed Jordan's King Abdullah while he visited the al-Aqsa (Dome on the Rock) Mosque in Jerusalem. His assailant was a young Palestinian extremist acting out his fear that the king—a moderate among other Arab leaders—would make a separate peace pact with Israel. The investigation that followed revealed eight or nine lawyers and prominent doctors behind the assault. They were all hanged.

The king's assassination triggered yet another war. As it raged around them, Hanna and his wife, Sarah, took in refugees from Haifa and other areas in far worse shape from the war than they were. The Farhat family moved to the first floor and let the refugees use their second floor until they found a permanent place to live.

There were many air raids, and one time a few bombs landed close to their house, shattering all the windows. Fortunately it was a well-built structure and no one was injured. While the war raged on, bombings became more frequent. Many people were killed, and sometimes entire villages were wiped out by both sides of the battle.

Palestinian property fell victim to theft as well. The Farhats owned a large orange grove with nearly 400 acres of highly productive trees. The Israelis seized the grove and took it for themselves, although the ownership papers clearly displayed the Farhats as the legal owners. The destruction continued and Hanna waited for the opportunity to send his daughters to America. When his mother passed away, he decided it was time to leave.

Hanna's daughters, Abla and Lamya, were in their mid-teens, and as it turned out his timing was good. If they wanted to enter the U.S. as legal immigrants, they would have to go soon in order to arrive below the maximum age requirement. The reason is when Hanna was in the States, he established citizenship for his three children under the visa policy that stipulated the children would have to enter the U.S. *before* their sixteenth birthday. If not, they would lose the opportunity. So in 1952, Abla and Lamya sailed for America. Hanna and Sarah would soon follow, but that would mean they had to leave their big, beautiful home behind.

They didn't want to sell it, nor could they leave it empty; an empty home invited strangers to move right in and abuse the property. The solution was to donate the house to the city of Ramallah to be used as a center for boy and girl scouts to learn art, music, swimming, and so on. Their decision was right; since Hanna's family left, the house has been in continuous use the way the Farhats intended. As of May 2016, when John's sister Abla traveled to Ramallah, she reported the house was in beautiful shape and the third and fourth generation of boy and girl scouts continue to enjoy the facility.

By 1956, about one fourth of Ramallah's 6,000 natives—many of the Orthodox Christian faith—had left. Many of them went to the open arms of America, and not a few found temporary refuge at the home of John Farhat.

Chapter 2

Pin Monkey to Line Worker

Ramallah immigrants did not fit the typical refugee mold. These were mostly educated, motivated people with enough foresight to know their life would never be the same. Instead of being thrown from their homes by the ravages of war, they chose to create their own future beforehand by embracing the opportunities available in the west. When they arrived, they did whatever they could to earn a living instead of relying on handouts from the government. If they received any sustenance, it was fully appreciated and used only until they could find a way to take care of themselves. For the most part, newly arriving immigrants received help from other transplanted families from Ramallah.

When John arrived he had less than $200 in his pocket and he didn't know the language. He landed jobs washing dishes at pizzerias, and even worked as a "pin monkey" at a local bowling alley. Eventually, his father and another friend helped him get a job at one of the Ford plants in the area. Ford had just re-tooled from making Jeeps and other war machinery, to new passenger car models for the blossoming American post-war population.

John also became friends with the Syrian community in Detroit—fellow immigrants with a similar background who arrived years before. They knew the ropes of American life and took John, their "skinny little kid," under their wing to help him get started. He became close friends with several Syrians, and remained so for the rest of his life. Over the next several years, John worked, saved, and planned for his next move.

***

With Jeanette's visa secured, she and her grandparents packed as much of her things as they could and prepared to leave. Like John, they boarded a cargo ship in Haifa bound for New York. John met them there, but instead of going back to Detroit they went straight south to Jacksonville, Florida, where several Ramallah immigrants had already settled. It was 1955 when John and Jeanette moved into their first home in the north side of the city.

Chapter 3

The North Side

The Jacksonville of 1955 was vastly different from today. There were no high-rises, no shopping centers, and only three bridges spanned the St. John's River. Four-prop TWA Constellations landed at the Jacksonville airport, and a railroad passed right behind the control tower. Shoppers spilled into the streets of Jacksonville's downtown area, and cars drove right onto the beach at the end of Atlantic Boulevard to avoid the summer heat. Piggly Wiggly was the food store of choice.

On the broader scene, Dick Clark became host of American Bandstand, and Elvis Presley would soon perform at the Florida Theatre. That was the year he released, "Don't be Cruel" and "Hound Dog"—both number-one on the charts. The "I Love Lucy" and "The Ed Sullivan Shows" would become the hottest American TV entertainment. That was the year the Soviet Union's Nikita Khrushchev pounded his shoe on the desk declaring, "We will bury you!" while in the Middle-East, Egyptian president Nasser pledged to "reconquer Palestine." With that as his backdrop, John went right to work at a local Pic-N-Save store until he earned enough money to open his own establishment.

During their years living and working in the Northside, Jeanette bore four children. First came Cindy, followed by Johnny, Jack, and then Abraham (Abie). Seemingly all at once the couple had four kids with three in diapers, and all before Jeanette reached the age of 21. Their fifth

Life before children - 1955

John's former store on Moncrief Boulevard – bought in 1954

child, Eddie, was born four years later. Eddie tragically passed away at a young age, an event to be discussed later. John and Jeanette's eldest child and only daughter, Cindy, recounted her early days in the north side.

"I remember we had a little house on West 23rd Street near the downtown area. It was just a little box, a one story stucco house. There were no hallways, so when you entered the living room you'd walk through to the other areas. We used the dining room as a place for a sofa and the TV. There was only one TV in the house, and it had a round black and white screen with rabbit ears for an antenna. We had a long, narrow kitchen, and two bedrooms were connected to that, but you had to go through our only bathroom to get to the third bedroom."

Meanwhile, Ramallah immigrants continued to stream into various parts of the U.S. Eventually their numbers would reach about 45,000, with ten percent of them in Jacksonville proper. Other areas they chose were San Francisco, Detroit, Houston, Washington DC, and Chicago. Now that John and his father were well-known in both Ramallah and Jacksonville, many newly arrived immigrants bound for Jacksonville sought their help. In fact, before some of them left Ramallah, John often wrote letters to the immigration officials saying he would sponsor them.

"After my brothers were born," continued Cindy, "a total of nine of us lived in that house. When people arrived from Ramallah, my parents allowed them to stay until they got on their feet. Although our house was really small, having them as guests was not a big deal as long as they were working and didn't get into trouble. For a while, it seemed like we hosted *everybody* that came from Ramallah. My brothers and I pretty much slept on the carpet in one of the rooms or anywhere else we could. Our dad was just that way … always giving a helping hand."

"I remember when my grandmother wanted to buy a washing machine," she continued, "because they washed all their laundry by hand. Can you imagine doing that for all the people we had living with us? Anyway, my grandfather said they didn't buy anything on loan, so they continued to wash by hand until they paid off the house. Only then did they buy the first washing machine. It was one of those round ones

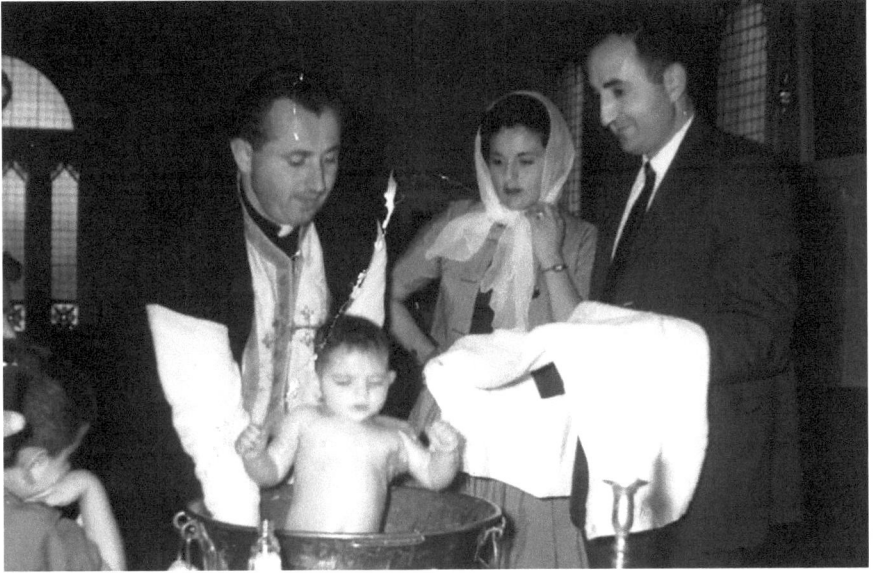

Baptizing their Godchild, Gina – early sixties

with the four wheels to roll it around, and had the two wide rollers to wring out the clothes. I used to play with it and one time I got my hand stuck between those rollers."

By the time Hurricane Dora hit Florida in 1964, John had built a little meat market and grocery store business (among his other talents, John was a butcher). Dora raked the Jacksonville area and took out most of the Atlantic Hotel and pier at the beach. It also erased all the power throughout the city for several days. Since the meat in his coolers would go bad, John loaded his truck with everything from the store that was perishable and brought it home. Everybody pitched in, fired up the grills, and started cooking all that meat. When it was done, he passed it out to their friends and neighbors. He literally fed the entire neighborhood with everything in the store that was perishable.

"Right after the hurricane," said Cindy, "my father installed a gas stove, saying he never wanted to be in the position again when he would have no electricity. Later, when he built our new house on the west side, he made sure we had both a gas kitchen *and* an electric kitchen … just in case."

John's third child, Jack, also remembered life on the Northside.

"It was a good time growing up there," he said. "We had a very close family and were pretty carefree. When I was a kid, every now and then I would go to my Dad's store and get some free bologna. He'd carve off a chunk from that big roll and give it to me."

"We all worked hard, sometimes as much as 18 hours a day, so there were times we didn't see as much of him as we'd like. But he really provided for us, and we always had food on the table. Mother didn't work outside of the house so she could look after kids. That was nice since she was always at home to take care of us."

Although the Farhat family acquired their father's strong work ethic, they still found time to enjoy themselves.

"Dad used to take us fishing once in a while," said Jack. "You know, we'd go off and do stuff like that, but it was more than just fishing. Our fun activities centered on doing things with the family, like spending time down at the lake having cookouts and things like that. We went to Gold Head State Park, Kingsley Park, or Strickland's Landing. Those times were good, but for the most part, with all the work and Dad's desire to help people coming from Ramallah, there wasn't much time for leisure."

***

During the years they lived on West 23rd Street, the Farhats managed to save a bit of money. Sensing an opportunity to earn extra income and regain some space in their crowded home, John bought the vacant lot at the end of their street and proceeded to build a six-unit apartment building. When they were done, John's parents moved in to one of the units. But they only slept there. In typical Ramallah family fashion, his parents spent the day and part of the evening with the rest of the family. Nevertheless, the extra space in the main house helped a lot.

Jeanette's mother-in-law, Sarah, was a huge help for the couple. By the accounts of the children and grandchildren, she was really good with them too. They said she was very intelligent and always made them laugh … a person they loved to be around. Apparently she was a great gardener too, which is where John acquired his green thumb.

"You know," said Jeanette, "when we first got married I was young and I thought I wasn't supposed to have the in-laws living with us. But they were very good people, and I cannot deny it was a big help for me to have my mother-in-law so close. She was the best. Just to have someone in the house with you all the time when you're young was good, but honestly, sometimes bad too. Of course when I get older, all that faded away. I did a lot in my life with her … a lot."

Cindy remembered just how close they became over the years.

"My mother and grandmother were like a team. They hosted more dinner parties than anybody I know. Everything had to be in my grandfather's house because he was the oldest son in the community. And since he lived with us, our house hosted all the gatherings. It's a cultural thing, a Ramallah thing. If you had a sister living in Jacksonville and a

John and Jeanette's first home on W. 23rd St.

Silver Street apartments John built in the early 60s

brother, you had to stay in the home of the brother regardless of age. So we got a *lot* of visitors, and in that sense my mom has been a real queen. And as time went on, after her in-laws helped her out, she took care of them and continued to do so until their death."

When Jeanette's mother, Jamelia, immigrated from Ramallah with her two sons, she moved into one of their apartments, and the Farhat family grew another notch. John rented the remaining two-bedroom-one-bath units for $65 per month.

John went on to invest in another four-unit apartment building called River View, and it became Grandpa Hanna's job to collect the rent every month. Cindy went with him to help, and her job was to knock on the doors and get the money. Actually, Cindy was so good at it that Grandpa Hanna never had to get out of the car.

"Toward the end of our time on the Northside," said Cindy, "we'd gathered a lot of relatives. They lived all around, either on the Northside or over on Murray Hill. We helped each other out. We had so many friends or relatives passing through that one of our neighbors saw a business opportunity and converted her home to a boarding house. That way she could take in our family overflow and make extra money. When any of our friends from Ramallah or maybe Detroit (many of Dad's friends moved south where the weather was more like the Middle East), they usually stayed with us. If we had no space they'd rent a room across the street. That ended up working out well for everybody.

That was our life; we didn't know any different. If we all had to sleep on the floor, we just did it.

My Dad, He Was My World

As I was growing up, everywhere Dad or grandfather went they would take me along. I was like their little monkey, or a little baby doll to them. There are many pictures of me standing on a table

---

dancing, wearing red velvet dresses, or other fun outfits. I remember I would always be with Dad. If he'd go for a walk, I'd be with him.

Every week, he would have to go drop the order off to Banner Food Store. He never could go unless I was in the car with him, because I went with him everywhere he went. And my grandfather too, he wouldn't go on a single errand unless I was with him in the car, like going to collect the rent from our tenants.

My dad was the only son and like all Arabs, particularly the men, they want a lot of sons. So when the phone call came from the doctor after my mother gave birth to me, my aunt was at the house and happened to answer the phone. Holding her hand on the receiver, she asked my family: "What do you want … a boy or a girl?" Everybody said, "A boy." When my grandfather heard the word, "boy," he got down and kissed the ground because he was so thankful. But then my aunt said, "Sorry, it's a girl." When Grandfather heard that he got up and said, "What is this, a curse?" Later he came up with a nickname for me: *Sodah Alahtma*, meaning "Dark of night" … like I was some kind of a curse. But the name stuck. "Hey Sodah," they'd call me. But it was really an endearing name, and I knew that. What is interesting is at first I really was considered a curse, because Mom had a miscarriage before I was born so it was even more critical for her to have a son. Well, their firstborn turned out to be a girl, but the funny thing is right after me, she popped out four sons in a row! That's when I wound up being good luck after all.

The night before my grandfather died, I went to the hospital to see him. He called me Sodah again. And just before my dad died, he called me that name too.

Cindy Gazaleh

Chapter 4

Building for the Future

Although he left the Middle East, John never really separated himself from his roots and the land he loved. Even at age 14, when he went to America, the call to walk in the furrows of a Ramallah garden and knead the soil with his hands was a big part of his life. According to a lifelong friend, Samir Farhat, John was an outgoing child who loved nature. Eight years his senior, John was also Samir's big brother with whom he played a lot of games.

"He always seemed to be outdoors doing something in a field or a garden," said Samir, "and he loved all kinds of animals. It was in his blood."

When John and his wife arrived in the Northside it was already a well-developed part of the city. That's where all the people were, and where there were people there was commerce. But he longed for a plot of land to grow things, and maybe have a few animals like they did in Ramallah where his family owned that grove of oranges they sold throughout Palestine. Even Grandmother Sarah had a garden on a little piece of land behind her apartment where she grew almost everything. She had her friends bring seeds back from Ramallah when they returned from a trip. When she planted them, they seemed to grow like crazy.

Now that he'd established himself as a viable, relatively prosperous citizen, John began to look at other areas of Northeast Florida where he could stretch out on real soil. Several parcels of land were available on the west side of Jacksonville around a two-lane road called Normandy Boulevard. There were no gas stations, hardware stores, or even restaurants (not that the Farhats ever ate out), so land was for sale at a good price. John saw the opportunity and bought as much as he could. At first he didn't do anything with it, but the fact that it was there gave him peace of mind, knowing there was a place he would someday watch his family grow. He wouldn't know how timely his decision was.

A Force Majeure

Jacksonville had long been a racist city. By the 1960, the ratio of black to white had reversed from a majority of blacks to a majority of whites by a wide margin. Unfortunately, the more the white population grew, the more the black population saw their rights diminish. Then in 1960, two events triggered a string of violent interracial acts that would span several years.

The first happened in August of that year, when protests against segregated lunch counters at the Woolworth's, McCrory's, and Kress stores turned ugly. There were several fights and many blacks were arrested and jailed. The next day, two black youths accidentally knocked a white woman into a plate glass window prompting more fighting. Later that month, hundreds of Ku Klux Klansmen demonstrated in downtown Jacksonville, but all the police did was stand by and observe while the blatant racist activities went on. Then on August 27, several black patrons again staged sit-ins at the lunch counters of Woolworth's and Morrison's Cafeteria. Not only were they refused service, they were attacked by around 200 middle-aged white men wielding axe handles. The result was fifty injured and one shot among a crowd of 3,000. Jacksonville's infamous "Axe Handle Saturday" became one of the worst racial violations of the era.

Four years later on February 16, 1964, a bomb exploded in the downtown Jacksonville home of a civil rights worker. No one was hurt, but the incident sparked a fresh round of riots. The unrest continued throughout the sixties, ebbing and flowing with each violation. When the Rev. Martin Luther King was assassinated on April 4, 1968, rioting spread not only throughout Jacksonville's Northside, but the entire country. By then, John's store and meat market had been ransacked several times. Windows were broken and merchandise was stolen. While that went on, more and more immigrants continued to arrive from Ramallah as a result of the 1967 Arab-Israeli Six-Day War. Now John and Jeanette's home was busier than ever.

Since the Farhats lived near "ground zero" of the city's civil rights chaos, John knew they would have to move soon. Fortunately, he began buying his property on the West Side in the early sixties and started construction on their new home. It was a cash-and-carry project, so progress was slow. However, after yet another break in at his store he decided to move immediately. He simply closed the doors to his shop, gathered his family, and left everything behind. Cindy remembers it well.

"My grandfather picked us up and we just left. It was a little scary. We never saw the inside of our house again. Sometimes today if I'm back in that neighborhood I'll go by for a look. There were a lot of good memories there."

We yanked his hair out

Growing up, our Dad was firm but he was also fair. And he always wanted to help us out with anything. When we lived on the Northside, one of my jobs was to put the groceries on the shelves. Dad had an employee named Sherman who also helped stock shelves and things like that. After a while, it got to a point where my parents were scared for me to work at the store because they started getting robbed a lot. It finally got so bad that my dad just left the store with some of the guys who helped him run it.

He just left at all to them. He was pretty generous, you know.

I remember before he got into this business we used to go fishing every once in a while. He didn't have a lot of time because he worked almost every day, but he still managed to take us. We also went on a vacation every year, and went to the same place in Winter Haven called the Shamrock Hotel. That was our big thing every year. I remember when I was seven or eight and we took swimming lessons there. We were so frightened of getting dunked that we would grab hold of Dad. He had a lot of hair on his chest and when we grabbed him we yanked a lot of his hair out. It was a lot of fun.

Dad drove an old mint green Ford Galaxy station wagon that used to give him a lot of problems. We'd jump in he took us everywhere in that thing. It was the only car we had until later, when my mom got a little Chevy Corvair. That was her first car, and she parked it in front of the house until one day someone ran around the corner and totaled it.

Johnny Farhat

With all five children - mid-sixties

With Eddie at the Shamrock Hotel

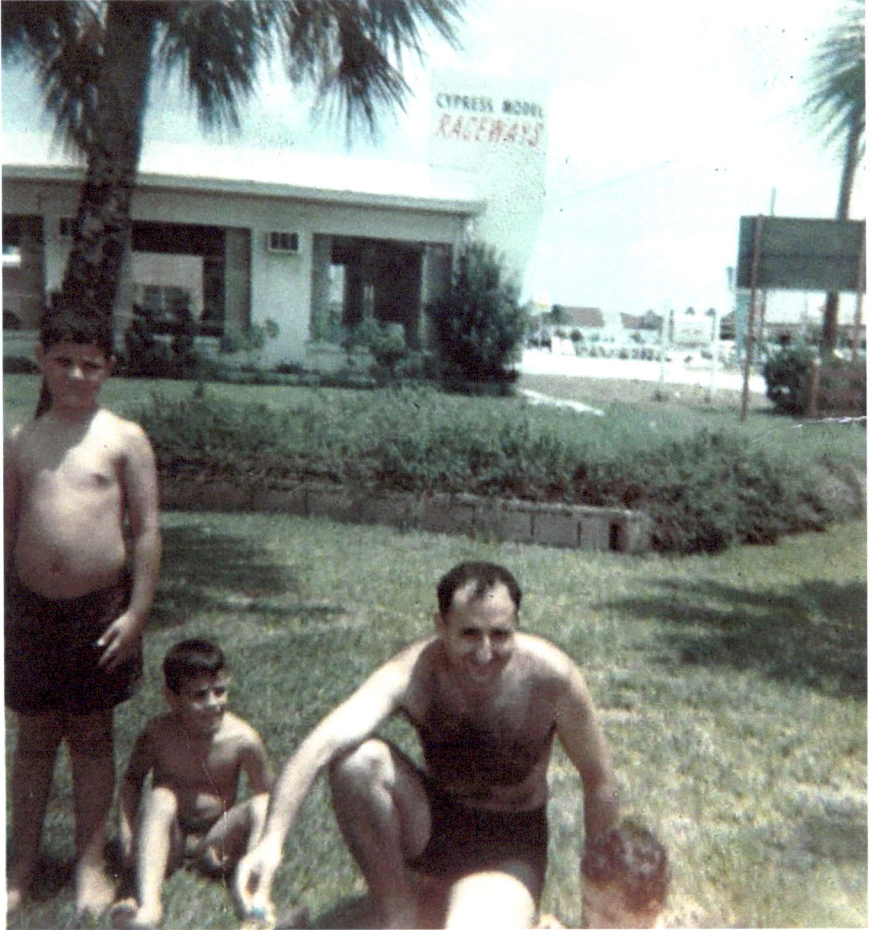

The Shamrock Hotel

Chapter 5

The West Side

To keep the family safe, John pulled up roots and moved his family into their partially constructed home off Normandy Boulevard. Some slept on beds in rooms waiting to be sheet rocked or paneled, while others slept on the floor with only a rug between them and the cold cement. In a way the relative discomfort was not unlike what they had on the Northside, except there were no shouts of violence or gunshots ringing through the neighborhood. Once the family settled in however, it didn't take long for John to grow weary of what amounted to a retired lifestyle.

"He was okay for maybe three weeks," recalled Cindy, "but my mom was going crazy. All he wanted to do was go to the grocery store. That went on and on, and he kept buying stuff until my mom told him he had to get out and do something. The next thing we knew, he started building a little convenience store in front of the house."

The original ten acres John bought was enough for their house, the store, and a good-sized garden plot nearby. It turned out that convenience store was the humble beginning of Green Ares Sporting Goods, which over the years would expand six or seven times.

When they first moved in there was a little run-down beer joint on the other side of the boulevard from their home … a real dive that looked like it had been there forever. On most weekends around closing time, the drunks wandered out of the bar and often wound up on the Farhat's

With Angie: the first girl born in the family since Cindy

front lawn. They were loud and potentially dangerous, particularly since their children's rooms faced the street and were accessible to anyone coming near. Whenever they came on the Farhat's property, John would haul out his 12-gauge and fire a couple of rounds in the air. That took care of the problem for the time being

The Farhats didn't leave the Northside only to have the same kind of danger come at them from right across the street every weekend. So one day John solved the problem for good. When he found out the bar was for sale, he jumped right in and bought it. It isn't clear whether there were other buyers or if he made them an offer they couldn't refuse. Either way, the day after they consummated the sale, John hired a friend to bulldoze the entire establishment. One day the kids came home from school and the old bar was nothing but a vacant lot. The view of the other side of the street was better, and John knew his family would be safe once more.

Whenever a piece of property became available, whether connected to his property or close by, John bought it. First he acquired an acre between a neighboring church and their house, and as more acreage came available, he bought it up. That went on for a few years until John garnered around 50 acres, including 25 where their store is today, and the corner of Hammond and Normandy Boulevards. He also owns all the property from Normandy to Herlong Road at the local airport. Today, all the major intersections around them belong to the family, including that former bar across the street. With all that land, it's not surprising how the name "Green Acres" came about.

The Garden and the Store

Before the Farhats arrived, the land now occupied by their store and home was mostly swamp. Over time though, the whole family including kids and grandkids old enough to pick up a shovel, redeemed the land for better use. John arranged for multiple truckloads of dirt—50 or 60 loads at a time—to help fill in the low areas. They cut almost all of the trees down and stacked old car tires around the stumps to burn them out.

Environmental issues aside, that's how the land was cleared and the labor for all of it came from within the family.

The older children worked on the property most weekends and after school. The rest of them pitched in when they could, and everyone worked until dinnertime when Jeanette had prepared a meal big enough to feed a platoon. Homework came afterwards.

If it was hard work, it was family work, and each of John's children and grandchildren have fond memories of those times. When asked if it kept them out of trouble, Cindy replied, "Where would you go to get in trouble? There was nothing around us … only three small houses next to the store. It was a fun way to grow up."

John's "garden" grew into a small farm that included cows, a pen full of pigs, goats, chickens, and even a horse. The produce coming out of their acreage supplied enough food for family, neighbors, and even friends back in the Northside. The kids—mostly Cindy—used to ride their horse around the property since there was plenty of space to roam without worrying about being run over by a car. Technically it was Cindy's horse because as she said, "I was the only one that got a horse because I'm the only girl. I got whatever I wanted."

At one point John's farm boasted over 200 head of sheep. To keep them fed, John or his father went to the farmers market every morning and gleaned all their old produce—especially cabbage—but anything else they wanted to get rid of at the end of the day. The kids would sit on the fence and cut up chunks of cabbage, lettuce, carrots and whatever else they had, and feed it to the animals.

Occasionally the cows would get out of the yard, and neighbors would knock on their door to complain. When that happened, some of the kids formed a posse, spread out, found the missing cows, and herded them back home. They suspected a local old man up to some mischief let them out in the first place. They eventually hired a real cowboy who lived nearby on Crystal Springs Road to take care of the farm. If the animals needed something like shots or special grooming, he took care of it.

In the garden with Eddie – 1977

"Mom put me in a headlock"

My father was a very hardworking, honest man who treated everybody well. And treating everybody equally and fairly is what really established this business. If you ask a thousand people who walk in the door of Green Acres, that's what they would tell you. Dad was very humble and kept a low profile. He did his job and kept his nose to the grind stone. He's the one who gave us our good work ethic, and we're all trying to carry it on.

He was a very serious, you know ... very old school. He came from the old country so he was pretty strict on our upbringing. He didn't put up with any stuff over here and we learned to accept that. When he had to lay down the law, he'd lay down the law. We knew where we stood.

As for spankings, oh yeah, we got them back in the day. But it did us no harm, and we had it coming most of the time. It definitely works, compared to what's going on today. He would get mad at small things, but if it were something major he would talk to us and explain how we messed up. Those are the things I remember more than the whippings, because whippings would come and go. But when he talked to us it was different. He did it calmly, and it really got through to us. When we got little older, it worked even better.

Mom was very loving and very nurturing. And she always wanted to feed us. I remember as a kid she would get hold of me in a headlock and shove food in my mouth. She wouldn't stop until I finished everything. It wasn't a matter of, "I'm not eating this or that"—she just made sure we ate it all. That was important to her. She wasn't like today's moms where with every little thing she had to run to the pediatrician. She took good care of us, and raised all of us in without any hassles. I think parents knew more back then than they do today when everyone relies on books, magazines, and the Internet. They learned all that stuff from their parents.

Jack Farhat

As the years passed, the Farhat family worked hard, grew up, and thrived. Their garden expanded, the farm prospered, and through fits and starts, John gradually built his business. His original 1,000 square-foot convenience store expanded to include feed and other supplies. Not long after he opened though, a Lil' Champ convenience store popped up nearby. Seeing his business dwindle, he converted the shop to a hardware store to cater to the needs of their growing community. Within a year however, an Ace Hardware store showed up less than a mile away. When Ace took his business, John sensed a niche in another growing market: guns and hunting equipment. Until then the only stores that sold guns were hardware stores. Since he already owned one, and Ace did not proffer firearms, he added a little glassed-in showcase and stocked a few of the more popular guns. They sold well. Then he added more, and different brands, which also sold. Now he was on to something. It seemed that soon as he stocked his store with this brand or that line, they quickly sold out. John's penchant for maximizing opportunity came through once again.

Every time he changed businesses, the original convenience store grew. First, from 1,000 square feet to 2,000. Then a new wing was added bumping it up to 5,000 square feet. That went on several times until the hardware gave way to guns, sporting, and hunting equipment. John's business became the first gun specialty outlet in the area. Green Acres Sporting Goods was born.

Chapter 6

Everybody Pitched In

When it comes to business, the Farhat family agrees on most everything. But there is one unwavering principle they all rally around: the family must stay together.

"The thing my dad wanted," said Johnny, "was for all of us to stay close and always be together, knowing the most important thing we had was each other. And that wasn't just our immediate family either. We had aunts, uncles, and cousins living on the other side of town. When they came out to see us, it was like an adventure. We'd burn tires and stumps, work in the farm or the store, and also play a lot. It was a long way from where they lived in the Brentwood area on the Northside to our place, so it was an all-day event including lunch *and* dinner. That happened mostly on Saturdays."

Like all family members, Phillip Gazaleh, started working in John's garden at the age of three or four where hard work, punctuality, teamwork, and an appreciation for the dollar took root. And like all the others, he eventually worked his way into the store when he was around twelve. By then he was old enough to know where things were and could help customers. John didn't want to give the customers bad information, so even at that age he had to know his stuff."

Brothers, sisters, aunts, uncles … everybody designated to work in the store began with the same tools and routine: a broom and a large

Cousins day at the Farhat farm

bottle of Windex. They started from the front doors where they sprayed, wiped, and swept, and worked their way back. If a customer asked a question, they put the bottle and broom down and courteously showed them where they needed to go. At the wiping and sweeping age, the kids couldn't actually sell to a customer, they only showed them where to go.

Once inside, Phillip discovered he was good with people, and very good at sales. That was fortunate because his grandfather didn't have to look over his shoulder all the time to see how he worked. But he did keep an eye on him from a distance. Over time, Phillip's work progressed into a career, as it did for most of the family.

"His only goal was to make sure the customer was taken care of," said Phillip, "to make sure we were fair to them, and courteous, and always gave the deal we told them we would give. And he always told us to smile, which was very important. That was the number one goal."

The only time John gave them strong, unwavering guidance was if he thought they weren't treating the customer with respect.

Buddy Gazaleh, Cindy's husband, is old enough to have watched the enterprise blossom from a convenience store to what it is today. During his student years, he worked at Green Acres part time, usually on Saturdays and Sundays. When they had a good day, John would slip him a few extra bucks. Buddy also noted how John handled transactions: whether it involved small change or large sums of money, he did it with ease.

"John took chances," said Buddy. "Sometimes he borrowed hundreds of thousands of dollars ... against his father's will. Hanna was a conservative old man who didn't believe in taking chances. But that's how it was in the old country, and he didn't realize the advantages of credit available in America. But John did, and he also had a vision for the future of his business. He was not afraid to borrow $200,000 or $300,000 to expand the enterprise. When he found out, Hanna would throw his hands in the air and say, 'My son borrowed $200,000 and now he got a computer. He want to run his business with a computer! They didn't do that in the old days, you know.'"

Jeanette worked with John in the store before the kids were old enough to help out. She put in lots of hours in addition to all else she did as a wife and mother. She'd get up in the morning, sometimes at two a.m., and go to the store with John where she'd sweep the floor, mop it, and organize the clothing line. She was done by seven a.m., so everything was ready to go when they opened the store at eight. Before the first customers walked in, she left the store and walked back to their home next door to start cooking lunch. Sometime around noon, she'd carry several dishes of homemade food back to the store where the family took shifts to eat. So much for the first half of the day. After lunch, she went back home, washed the dishes, and ran several loads of laundry. Then it was time to start dinner. It was a good thing she married so young: the sheer energy to do all that would call for three people under different circumstances.

For several years Jeanette was in charge of the store's clothing line. She initiated it in the first place, and over time became very good at it. She accompanied John to the trade shows where they bought "tons of clothing" that sold quite well. They went "all over the place," to Las Vegas, Houston, and even Germany. Their kids weren't old enough to help out, so John and Jeanette left them with their grandparents while they traveled the buying circuit. Since it was Jeanette's inspiration, she bought all the pants, coats, vests, and hats while John took care of guns and everything else.

"It was enjoyable," said Jeanette. "One time we found a line of children's clothing at a show, so we bought a ton of them and sold every one. I mean hundreds and hundreds of pieces, and with a good price on them. But John said, 'if you buy them, where we gonna put them?' I said we'd put them in the attic upstairs. So we brought them and we filled up the whole attic. Small camouflage jackets and pants for small kids. Later when we went to a show downtown, we took a lot of that clothing, and you should see those kids—they loved them, and their parents loved them too. Everybody wanted to buy them an outfit. They cost me maybe three or four dollars each and I sold them for $10 apiece.

John and Jeanette's anniversary – 1976

They moved like a hotcakes! So I said to John, 'I told you, see how they're moving?' We sold every bit of them, and I think I made more money on the clothing than anything else in the store."

However, the clothing success meant even more work for Jeanette's day. By around two or three in the afternoon—after cooking, doing the dishes and the laundry—John might call her up. "Where you at?" he'd say. That meant he needed her to take care of the clothing line, maybe to pull some out of the storeroom or make out a purchase order for popular-selling items.

"He couldn't do without me," said Jeanette, "because I had to be there to sell them. I worked *hours* with him … just me and him … we worked so hard before the kids took over. Sometimes when I get mad at him in the store with so much to handle, I said 'I am leaving.' Then I would go, just leave and go shopping to spend a little money. When I came back, everything was all right again. That's my weakness, just to get out for a little while."

Jeanette's virtual full-time work at the store came to an end around 25 years ago. By then the kids were firmly established in the store and she and her husband's stamina began to wane. A little later, Jeanette stopped working in the store altogether after their youngest son, Eddie, passed away.

I Couldn't Wear Short Shorts

I was a very strong girl. I guess because I grew up with four adults and I was the oldest of five siblings. When it came to my brothers, my dad taught me to be tough. "Don't let them get you," he'd say. Growing up, I was super, super skinny and when my brothers and I got into a fight; I just sat on the couch and started kicking them. Ask any of them. I used to get them on the ground and started beating them with my heels. But they couldn't get me because, well, I was Daddy's girl. I remember when they used to make trouble, they'd run down the road but I'd catch up and push them on the ground. I started screaming for somebody to come get them. I would just sit on them yelling until someone came.

My father was really tough on education. If my brothers came home with a 'C' grade, they were like, thanking God they even passed that year. But if I came home with a 'B' grade, they wanted to know why I only got a 'B,' and I would get in trouble.

He was also very strict with my clothing. I couldn't wear short shorts, and I couldn't wear short skirts. One time I was all dressed up to go to a wedding in a beautiful dress my mom bought me. When I got in the car, the dress scooted up above my knees and my dad said, "Get out of the car and stand up. I want to see what you're wearing." I got out in the driveway in my brand new dress (I was about 12 or 13 years old and looked so cute) and he goes, "Go back in the house ... you're not going." He was very protective over me."

Cindy Gazaleh

A Record Turkey

My grandfather loved hunting, and his big passion was hunting down turkeys. He went a lot until he got to the age when he just really couldn't do it anymore. Right up until a few years ago he held the record for the biggest turkey taken in the state of Florida. I think it's still number two or number three, but when he held the record, he did for fourteen years. That's a long time. It was a big deal when he landed that turkey and made the paper. That might be just a small blip on the radar for his life story, but he held the state record for that long. That's just one of the things that he accomplished.

I do hunt but don't do a lot of fishing, except out in the pond behind Grandpa's house for bass or brim. Aside from that I turkey hunt and deer hunt. My brothers have hunted bear and stuff like that. I've never done that, but I'd like to one day. My dad, Abie, has been to Africa three times. I've been hunting with him several times, but not to Africa. We've been to Canada four or five times, Montana a few times, Nebraska a few times, Iowa, and Texas. So we have gone on a lot of trips. That's one of the great things about my dad; he always said "I want to go on trips with you now while I'm at the age while I can still do it. Because once you get up there in age, it depends on what kind of hunting you're doing. If we go on an elk hunt, you gotta be in shape for that because you're walking up the mountains in the high altitude, not just sitting there."

I can say my grandfather really trusted people, and he helped them out when he could. I had a cousin that had cancer and needed help, so my grandfather gave him a pile of money—I'm not sure how much, but it was a lot. He was also generous towards me, like when I worked at the store and we had a good day, he would reward me. Just like that. At the time I made about sixty dollars a day, and he'd hand me another fifty, just because we had a good day.

Z Farhat

John and Jeanette's 23rd anniversary

Chapter 7

More Weddings

"If Palestinian weddings would stop, so would our culture." -Anon

John and Jeanette's wedding took place in Ramallah, in the context of their ages old culture. So it follows that all the trappings of the courtship (all two weeks of it), the agreement, the ceremony, and the celebration afterward, followed the same script used by their forefathers with little variation. Fast forward decades later to the transplanted Ramallah culture in Jacksonville, Florida, USA. One would think the American influence might have tainted the ritual as one after another Farhat offspring got hitched. It did, but not to the extent one would think. Consistent with John and Jeanette's desire to keep the family together meant all the rituals and mores of their marriage culture should be lived out by their children and grandchildren. The following article describes what a Palestinian wedding is really all about.

Weddings, some of which are still practiced within our traditional communities, have been inspired by rational and ideological influences that are solidly embedded within Arab social values and mores and conventional beliefs. Weddings are an accumulation of rearing practices and moral ethics among the Arabs, both those living in the East within the confines of the Arab World, and those who are spread around the globe.

Wedding practices have been manifestly influenced by religious and social factors. Within the Christian culture, which was widespread in the Arab East before the dawn of Islam, marriage is a sacrament and is therefore indissoluble; it forbids divorce and remarriage for both men and women, and forbids polygamy, which is a practice sanctioned by the Muslim religion. This is done for many reasons: to preserve the balance between males and females within the population and to prevent girls from becoming spinsters, which might lead them to sexual delinquency, considered a taboo in our conservative communities that strictly forbid girls from practicing sex outside marriage.

A wedding is the most important occasion to perform many practices that cannot be realized outside the boundaries of this ceremony. It is considered a connection between families, based on a common understanding and mutual respect between the parents of the bride and groom. It therefore becomes an important occasion to "settle accounts" between families, clans, tribes and kingdoms. We oftentimes hear of marriages of convenience that were, and continue to be, arranged by the parents of the bride and groom for the purpose of serving commercial or business interests or other purposes, without investigating the compatibility between the bride and groom or seeking their consent.

By Na'ela Azzam Libbes – *This Week in Palestine*
 # 105 - January, 2017

To illustrate the above, two of the Farhat children and their spouses discuss their experience of Palestinian style courtship and marriage in today's America. Both represent second-generation immigrants, and their ceremonies might compare to the well-known "Big Fat Greek Wedding," Ramallah style.

Cindy said her husband, Buddy, was the only man she ever dated. She first noticed him one day during choir practice at their Antiochian Church. He walked in with an older woman who turned out to be his mother.

"His mom was eyeballing me from across the church ... or eyeballing the girls, we didn't know which. We were all laughing, saying she's trying to hook one of us up with her son."

During a break between songs, the girls in the choir tried to guess which one was her target. It turned out it was Cindy, and after church Buddy walked up to her and said 'hello.' But Cindy's parents wouldn't let her date him because they said she was too young. She was eighteen at the time. In fact, they said she couldn't date any man unless she was going to marry him. When it was clear they would marry, John kept a steely eye on them nevertheless.

"That's how strict they were. Boys couldn't even call my house. My brothers could date, and they went to the school dances and stuff like that, but not me. As his daughter, I couldn't do anything."

If she went to the church for a youth activity, one of her brothers had to go with her. One time they sent Abie, her younger brother, along in the car with her. Abie was all of fifteen and as she put it, "was just a young punk." As the story goes, as soon as they left the house Abie said, "Hey, I don't care what ya'll do, just stop at the convenience store and get me a pack of cigarettes and a six-pack of beer." Even when Cindy's friend and cousin, Sally, went with her to church, one of the little "punks" had to sit in the back seat to protect them.

That's how it went. Their "chaperone," who was nine years younger than his sister sat in the back of the car while Buddy and Cindy sat up front. It was the same when Cindy took Arabic classes at FCCJ. She had to take her very young brother, Eddie, with her to chaperone.

It would appear such restrictions were even more than what might have been in Ramallah. The reason could be that two sets of old school folks lived in their house: her parents and her grandparents. They were new to America, and the new country with all its free life and creativity probably scared them. As a result they might have dug in harder with their old way of doing things. That put a lot of pressure on their only daughter, but that was typical of the Ramallah community.

"One time I got in trouble," she said. "Looking back, it was real funny how it happened. It was two weeks before our wedding, and Buddy and I went out to eat. I forget where we went, but sometime during the meal his watch stopped and we were late … *legitimately* late. Then, coming back home we drove down the Interstate I-10 and missed the Normandy exit. We ended up coming back on Chaffee Boulevard, which took even more time. When we got to my house my dad was sitting in his pickup truck in front of the store waiting for me."

She was grounded for the two weeks, right up to the day of their wedding. Her father told her, "If you ever go out with him again, have him come to the house and meet with him here where we can keep an eye on you." Then, as if to guarantee chastity prior to the wedding day, he told Buddy, "If you're going to marry her, that's fine. But until you do, she's still my daughter and I want her here. Once you're married, I'll never tell you what to do again."

John kept his word. From the day of the wedding onward, he never meddled into Buddy and Cindy's affairs. Buddy's perspective of their first encounter is slightly different.

"I first saw Cindy on a Sunday afternoon when I was twenty-five. My parents asked me to go to church with them. I didn't really want to go, but when they told me there would be a picnic afterward at the Ramallah club I said okay. Sitting in the pew during the service, I looked around the choir at all the girls in robes singing. I noticed one girl in particular, so I turned to my mother and asked her who that girl was over there. I nodded in the direction of the choir."

His mother sat up straight and started looking at all of them. When they noticed his mother's scrutiny, the whole group began to flutter. When she finally saw the one Buddy meant she said, "That's Cindy, your Uncle John Farhat's daughter."

Buddy originally met John back in 1962 when Buddy's parents ran a store around the corner from John's establishment. Every time John drove past, he honked the horn. If they ran out of an item like a certain brand of cigarettes, Buddy would walk around the corner and swap one brand of cigarettes for the one they needed. But he only knew John and John's father, Hanna, not the wives or children … at least not yet.

"But I do remember her," said Buddy. "She must've been six years old, and I was about thirteen. She was a cute little girl."

After his mother told him who the girl was, Buddy's eyes roamed between the priest in the pulpit and a certain girl standing in the choir. Later at the Ramallah Club picnic, he found Cindy in a booth selling raffle tickets. Finding himself in a rare situation where the scrutinizing eyes of parents were engaged elsewhere, Buddy asked a cousin to introduce him to "that girl." He did, and after the brief introduction Buddy asked Cindy if she needed assistance selling tickets. It turned out that she did need help, so while they distributed tickets they got to know each other. That went on through the evening, and eventually Buddy managed to get Cindy's phone number.

Without her parent's permission, he started calling her. That continued for a while until word got back to his father—through her grandmother who overheard the conversations—that Buddy called without her parents knowledge. His parents told him Cindy's father thought he was too old for her, and to stop calling altogether.

He obeyed for an entire year. They met again at a New Year's Eve party in the Dolphin Room of the Gulf Life Tower in downtown Jacksonville. In the midst of the noise and celebration, Buddy went up to her and said hello. Cindy said, "You stopped calling me. Why?" He explained what happened, and once again they exchanged phone numbers. Now they talked *every day*. By then Cindy was nineteen and both of their parents were well aware of their mutual attraction, and communication. No one put a stop to it this time. Three months later Buddy's father approached him and said, "I think we need to go and visit her parents, don't we?"

Like Jeanette's grandfather many years before in Ramallah, in March of 1976, Buddy's father called John to say he wanted to visit with him over coffee. The words, "visit over coffee" was Palestinian code meaning it was time to visit the daughter and see if there is potential for marriage.

Buddy went with his parents and they spent the afternoon talking. Apparently it went well. According to Buddy, not long after the meeting Cindy informed her parents, "That's the guy I want to marry. If I don't marry him, I'm *never* going to get married!"

They all agreed it would be a good match. Then Buddy went by himself to Cindy's house and sat down in the low-ceilinged living room with her parents to talk. They passed the time with light conversation until Cindy's parents finally spoke to the elephant in the room.

"Okay," said John, "you can come here to visit but you can't go out with her."

They went out anyway. "But that happened only once," recalled Buddy, "before I actually asked for her hand in marriage." That was April, 1976, one month after that meeting with her parents. The good thing was Buddy had prior approval from Cindy's parents, so he didn't have to go through the customary querying of the father before popping the question.

She said 'yes' and like all Ramallah citizens they had a big engagement party. Theirs took place at the Normandy Boulevard National Guard armory on April 18th, Easter Sunday. Three months later on July fourth of that same year, they were married. Their wedding reception was typically huge. Everyone who knew anyone associated with the Gazaleh and Farhat family attended, compliments of the father of the groom.

Before the Ramallah community of Jacksonville built their new church on Bowden Road, the Antiochian members attended an old church on Hendrix Avenue they acquired after another denomination went out of business, so to speak. But the building was too small, so the families rented the St. John's Episcopal Cathedral on Church Street in Jacksonville for the wedding. It turned out well because it was the only cathedral in Northeast Florida, and the architecture was stunning.

The service was typically Orthodox, which meant very lengthy. The orthodox members knew what to expect, but their non-orthodox guests couldn't understand why it took so long for a couple to get married, and why they had to stand up and sit down so often. All Buddy and Cindy could do was tell them their church was similar to a Catholic or a Greek Orthodox service. In fact, the Antiochian church is not much different than a Greek ceremony, since the Greek church served as the primary source of worship in the early years of Ramallah. Much of their liturgy remained when the Antiochian Church came into being.

The preacher conducted most of Buddy and Cindy's ceremony in Arabic. But high church in a wedding, even for the staunchest parishioner, was difficult. Particularly for young people. As the eldest, Cindy was only nineteen, and the ages of four siblings went on down to ten years old. That became a recipe for boredom during a long ceremony. So when the lengthy singing mass began, some of the kids made up their own words instead of reciting the liturgy, just for fun.

"One of our cousins was a Catholic and he sat right behind us," recalled Cindy. "When the priest intoned his Latin sing-song, the kid kept singing, "Kumbaya, kumbaya." When the priest sang another term in Arabic meaning, "Lord have mercy," another cousin within earshot sang, "You're a boar hog … you're a boar hog!"

After they exchanged rings, Buddy and Cindy exercised one of the seven sacraments of the Church: a ritual found in most Orthodox churches throughout the world called, "The Crowning." During the ceremony, the priest placed a crown on the Buddy's head while reciting the "crown blessing" three times: "The servant of God, Buddy Gazaleh, is crowned unto the handmaiden of God, Cindy Farhat, in the name of the Father, and of the Son, and of the Holy Spirit. Amen."

Then the priest placed a crown on Cindy's head and recited the same crown blessing, but in reverse. "The handmaiden of God, Cindy

Gazaleh, is crowned unto the servant of God, etc." That done, the priest chanted, "Oh Lord our God, crown them with glory and honor." He said that three times while lifting up both crowns and switching them back and forth over the bride and groom's head. The two said it was truly a beautiful ceremony, amidst all the guests, incense, flowers, and vaulted ceiling of the cathedral.

Around 535 guests attended the reception in the Dolphin Room of the Gulf Life Towers on the river—the same place Buddy met Cindy on New Year's Eve. Open bars weren't in vogue then, so they compensated by placing bottles of liquor on the table with a variety of mixers. As the evening went on, it got even better because that day marked America's Bicentennial celebration. As if to crown Buddy and Cindy's wedding, spectacular fireworks exploded over the river followed by a long, colorful boat parade. Cindy recalled sitting in her wedding dress on the grass in front of the hotel with Buddy watching the show. There was no Riverwalk then, so everyone had gathered to watch along the riverbank.

As mentioned earlier, in Ramallah the groom's family paid for the wedding dress and that's how it was with Buddy and Cindy. Her dress cost over a thousand dollars, and her headpiece alone went for around $1500. In 1976 dollars, that was a lot.

"It was a beautiful reception," said Cindy. "It was just so much fun because people from outside were coming in and having cocktails with the guests. That's where everybody in Jacksonville used to go to watch the fireworks and we were right on the water in the middle of it all."

"There's always some turmoil during the planning of the wedding," said Buddy, "between the girl's family and the boy's family. One side says they want this many people invited, and the other side says they want that many people. But with our wedding, my father-in-law said, "Your father and I never disagreed on anything. Of course, your (Buddy's) father had to pay for everything for the wedding, so I concurred with everything he said." He laughed. "But we just got along so good."" In actuality, Buddy's father and John really did get along well.

Cindy got pregnant right after the honeymoon. Ten months later, they had their first son, Essa ... the Farhat family's pride and joy because he was their first grandchild. One day not long after Essa was born, John picked him up and proudly strutted around the Ramallah Club holding him high. At the time John was a very young 43-year-old grandfather who loved to show him off.

A Somewhat Arranged Marriage

If John's only daughter's marriage was a monumental event, Abie's marriage would be just as spectacular since he was the first of John's *sons* to get married. Although it took place just a few years later, it appears the rules of courting had eased significantly ... probably due to the "male factor." This time it was his son, so John could leave all the worry up to the parents of Abie's wife, Maysoon.

Maysoon lived in Arkansas with her parents at the time, and had visited the Farhats in Jacksonville. As the story went, John tried to set her up with Abie's older brother, Johnnie. When Maysoon showed up with her mother and uncle for lunch at the Farhat's house, Johnnie wasn't there, but neither was Abie—her future husband. According to Maysoon however, Abie's parents told him about her. "Abie," they said, "you should meet this girl. She's very cute." Apparently, Abie laughed and said he'd like to meet her. At first, he thought it was some kind of a gag since he and his grandfather tended to joke a lot. His grandfather would point his bony finger at Abie and say, "You're a coward ... you're a chicken ... you won't go meet anybody."

"No, I'm not a coward, this time I'll go meet her," said Abie. "Call them up and we'll go over to the house where she's staying."

His grandfather called up John to make the arrangement. They agreed to meet for coffee (there's that coffee meeting again) and that's when Maysoon met Abie. They were both twenty years old.

"My first impression of Abie was he looked like a bad boy. He sat and had a beer with my uncle and smoked a cigarette, and that was my first impression. He was real nice though, and he called me up and we went out."

According to Abie, it wasn't as simple as calling her up and going out. Like all Ramallah offspring, he had to walk a careful path to get permission in the first place.

"She was a pretty girl, so I kind of liked her from the beginning. But when it came to asking her out, it was one of those deals … you had to make sure everything was proper. You can't just say, 'You wanna go out?' It's got to be good with the parents before you can do anything."

Maysoon would only be in town a few weeks more before returning to Arkansas, so Abie timed the question very carefully. A few days after their first meeting, he called her parents and asked if he could take her out. According to Abie, her father was very nice about the whole thing … quite a difference from John's reaction to Buddy's initiatives. It also helped that her father knew the Farhats very well, so a degree of trust had already been established. They went out twice before Maysoon was due to go back home. But, after their second date, Abie asked her to marry him. She said 'Yes.'

"Are you kidding?" said Maysoon. "I think it was love at first sight with us. It must have been, we've been married for 35 years."

She and her family stayed another week so they could throw a big engagement party. After that, they went back to Arkansas. Five months later, they were married in Jacksonville. True to the Arabic tradition, the groom's father paid for the wedding.

"My dad wanted to throw a big one for his first son getting married," Abie said. "A new hotel had opened downtown, and because my dad always liked to do stuff first-class, he spent a bunch of money and threw a big wedding and invited everybody."

They held the reception at the newly built Sheraton Hotel on the riverbank. Around five-hundred attended and as usual, they enjoyed a full sit-down dinner with a lot of drinking, which was always part of a Ramallah celebration.

While Abie and Maysoon's marriage was not arranged, it came close. Behind each of them stood an army of parents, grandparents, siblings, and centuries of tradition compelling them to marry even if they didn't know the other very well. But it worked out of course. After 35 years, they have two children who in turn gave them two grandchildren. According to both, they are quite happy. Maysoon looks back at the family she married into.

"I love my in-laws! They took me into the family when I didn't really know anybody in Jacksonville except my uncle who lived here of course. And when you're young, you don't know much, really. But my in-laws accepted me, and became even more than parents. They were the nicest, especially my father-in-law. I could talk to him and tell him anything."

In these modern times, the institution of arranged marriage is in question more than ever. Not just those from Ramallah, but throughout the Arab world, India, parts of China, and so on. Nevertheless, arranged marriages are still considered successful and with time, may even develop into a loving relationship. Why is that? One answer may be that arranged marriages have lower expectations than 'love' marriages. After the wedding vows, the only way forward in an arranged marriage is up. An even stronger point is arranged marriages have firm roots in society and culture which makes it even harder to dissolve a relationship, even if troublesome problems emerge. It much more difficult to dissolve a marriage when surrounded by a host invested witnesses. Finally, the accumulated wisdom and council of two sets of parents (once a degree of freedom is relinquished to accommodate the newlyweds) helps let off steam when trouble arises.

"My father-in-law was unusually open and caring with me," said Maysoon. "I could talk with him about anything. During our first year of marriage, especially after meeting and marrying within six months, I didn't really know much about Abie. So we went through our ups and downs. The first year was kind of rough and we had a lot of fights. But with me, my father-in-law would always take my side ... not in front of my husband of course, because he never interfered. But, if I went to him with any questions, he was there to answer them. He always said, 'I'm here for you guys if you want to come ask me a question.' He would never butt-in and say, 'Why did you say this or why did you do that.'"

Semi-arranged or arranged marriages aside, if Abie and Maysoon ever wanted an in-house counseling service, John's wisdom and advice coupled with Jeanette's living example of complimentary partnering, proved the best way to insure a long-term, successful relationship.

With all his sons and "Z" at Eddie's wedding

Oldest son Johnny's wedding - 1984

Chapter 8

Life around the table

John loved his property. He had the means to live anywhere he wanted, and although there were several times Jeanette would have preferred to live near the beach or in a different neighborhood, he stayed at the Normandy Boulevard house because he wanted to keep the family together. So it followed that holiday gatherings were always at *his* house, and they always invited numerous people. It was nothing to have fifty or a hundred guests at their Christmas party or for Easter dinner. And Jeanette, with the help of other women, always did the cooking right at home.

"We ate mostly in the kitchen," said Phillip. "They would set up hors d'oeuvres that were almost as big as a regular meal. Everybody stood up to eat, almost like a food truck, and my grandmother would make the biggest feast … enough to feed a battalion. It was like an assembly line with the entire house full of people. I remember us kids just had a little table in the garage they'd converted into a kind of den area, and everybody would sit around and eat. As you got older you got to move into a room inside the house, and eventually you wound up in the actual dining area. Thanksgiving was traditional but most of the meals would be a lot of Arabic dishes like stuffed grape leaves, or stuffed squash picked fresh from the garden that morning."

As stated earlier, one Palestinian tradition meant everybody who was younger than the eldest brother went to his house for special holidays. Which is why everyone wound up at John and Jeanette's. Even if it wasn't a special occasion, they often went there anyway. They'd assemble in the morning for the first meal, and after that the younger parents took their kids around to the homes of another, younger family, or to a friend's house to wish them a happy holiday. Every house they entered had something for them: presents on Christmas, eggs or candy on Easter, special treats on Thanksgiving. As older parents, the Farhat children accompanied their dad on the rounds while the wives stayed home preparing for the rest of the family who would show up later. It was like a big progressive dinner that involved scores of relatives throughout the city, and lasted all day.

Like all hardworking wives, sometimes Jeanette lamented the extent of her labor. She recalled one instance when their children needed to show more appreciation for home cooked food.

"When my kids or my grandchildren came from school, they always find me home. So I always had food for them. We spent all our life saving to take care of the family, and I used to ask him (John), when is our turn gonna come? When will we have something for ourselves? And he said, 'Family comes first. We have to take care of the family.' And he did. All his life his family came first. And here it is, you can see what kind of family he raised. All our children and grandchildren under one roof. This is what he built."

Sometimes John and Jeanette had to show tough love when it came to being home on time. John always warned his kids that if any of them (the boys, not Cindy of course) came in after midnight that he wouldn't let them in the house. One time Jack and his friends were out drinking, and before they came home they decided to stop at the Famous Amos restaurant down the street and have an early breakfast When he finally got home around 1:30 AM, John said, "Go right back out where you were … you're not coming into the house."

As the story went, it was below freezing that night so Jack went around back to a garden shed and bunked out there. Jeanette heard about

Conducting his own birthday song

it, and after John went back to bed, she snuck out the side door and gave Jack a couple of blankets and a ten dollar bill. That's how Jack survived the rest of the night.

"John and I kept everything together through the years," said Jeanette, "and sometimes we went through hard time raising the family. The children also went through wrong things here and there, and we suffered for it. But John, he got them in the right place at the right time. He did everything for them. If it weren't for him, this family wouldn't be together, because I'm a little bit too weak, but he's a strong one. He was strict on them, but it paid. And spankings? Oh yeah. They get punished and sometimes they could not go out."

Wife of my Uncle

After we were married a while, we became like friends with Cindy's parents. We went out with them on vacation, since they wouldn't go with their sons. We didn't go with my parents because they were much older than us. But everywhere we went it was her parents and us, because we were more compatible. And the age difference; Cindy's mother is twelve years older than me so we were about the same age. They would call us and say, "Do you want to go and do such and such?" And I would always answer, "Who's paying?" Sometimes we would go to a casino, and John would slip $500 in my pocket.

One time we were heading to Biloxi and he wanted some liquor. So we stopped at a liquor store and he took a bill out of his pocket and said, "Go get us two big bottles of Crown." I looked and it was a twenty dollar bill. So I looked at her mother and I said, "He wants me to go get two big bottles with this?" And she said, 'John why you only give him

---

twenty? He thought he gave me a hundred, or so he said. We had a lot of stories of us together. He was like an older brother, but I respected him like a dad because he treated me real good.

I remember one time the electricity at my father's store went out. John brought his van from his store and loaded all the meat from our freezer and the cooler, put it in his van, and took it to his store until we had our refrigeration repaired. He did that without even asking. The minute he heard our electricity went out, he was there. And I know my father was very appreciative of that.

So I'm proud to say that I'm part of the family, and I've always respected them and looked up to them. They treated me like their sons, maybe even better. That might be because I married their only daughter, so I guess I'm the lucky one. At the time you know, they just felt like we were too young. But, anyhow it worked out really well.

John's life was around the grandkids, and the grandkids loved him. He also loved having everybody at his house. Ever since my parents passed away, that's the only place we go for Easter, Thanksgiving, Christmas. Everybody gets together and goes there.

John helped so many people in the Ramallah community in Jacksonville, and even relatives up in Michigan. When I say 'helped,' he did it financially, and he did it big time. He gave $100,000 or more at times, if someone needed help. They usually paid him back, but there was no guarantee he would ever get it back.

He and my mother in law are closer than family. I call John "*Ummo*," which means uncle, out of respect. In the Ramallah community, you call your elders Ummo. So I never referred to him as John, only *Ummo*. I refer to my mother-in-law as *Mart Amee*, which means "wife of my uncle." I never call her Jeanette, just *Mart Amee*. That goes on within the Ramallah community, but it's kind of dying these days. Young second-generation kids don't show that kind of respect that we did, because we're first-generation. My parents came here in in 1946, but my kids and other kids that age, they don't show the respect to their elders. They call them by their name or call them Mister.

Buddy Gazaleh

Thanksgiving -1978

Chapter 9

Inside Green Acres

New customers walking into Green Acres Sporting Goods immediately feel something different. Certainly the dozens of trophy animals sprouting from the walls around the perimeter are striking enough. Most of the trophies came from the Farhat family, but some came from good customers who might not have enough room in their house, or their wives didn't want sad deer eyes staring them down in their living room. There are whitetail deer, an elk, a turkey, a mule deer, and a great big bear. It's a hunter's paradise.

Once entering, if you look to the left you'll find long shelves and glass cases loaded with guns all the way to the left rear of the store. To the trained or untrained eye, they represent just about every legal brand and style of firearm imaginable. The lower walls on the right side of the store are lined with as many sport bows and arrows one could want. And down the middle, counter after counter is loaded with artifacts, accessories, manuals, guidebooks, and plenty of ammunition. One can buy all they need and want there. There is no doubt that Green Acres, with its 46 years of experience in the trade, carries everything a sportsman needs. There is even a concealed weapons certification course offered at the rear of the store at a very competitive price. The only stipulation is personal guns must be not be loaded when entering.

The store is packed with everything and the prices are competitive. But what makes Green Acres truly unique is the atmosphere of quiet competence one feels upon entering. If you look closely at the men and women behind the counters or leaning over to pick up a gum wrapper, you'll discover a distinct similarity in their features. That's because only one of the employees is *not* a family member. Talk about nepotism … John Farhat's business has to be one of the few successful enterprises where a very large family is completely in charge.

The staff also pays attention to their clients. John never let a customer walk out of the store without being served one way or another. If a customer bought a gun, John would say, "Hey, wait a minute … come over here." Then he'd hand him a free box of ammunition. John always gave them something and made sure everyone walked out satisfied. If a client was ever unhappy with a purchase, with no questions asked he would take it back and return their money.

Another unique attribute of Green Acres was the way John answered the phone. He did it for all the years he was there, and if anyone else tried it, they would come off as rude.

"Hello, Green Acres. How can I take your money please?"

That's what he said, and people loved it. His salutation became one of the store's hallmarks. Everyone who knows Green Acres—and they are myriad—jokingly refer to him as, "John-can-I-take-your-money-please." Those who knew him let it pass, but new ones to the store were immediately disarmed by his warm, Palestinian accent. After all, when anyone calls a place of business, unless they're a relative of an employee reminding them to pick up the milk and eggs on their way home, they expect to be sold on something. John simply cut to the chase, and in a lighthearted way took the tension out of the transaction. That line is literally known throughout the city: "Hello, can I take your money please?"

Green Acre's strong presence in the market is mostly due in part to their great customer service and low prices. While those words are used by every retail outlet around, they were absolutely true with John's business. One reason the "low prices" claim is valid, is Green Acres can withstand the ups and downs of the retail industry due to private ownership. They are not in debt as an organization because John never believed in debt in the first place. Z Farhat remembered his grandfather's philosophy on the subject.

"Most people take the money they earn and put it in the bank," said John, "but I reinvested it in the business." He went onto say, "You know, why do I need all this money? I make enough to put food on the table and pay my bills, but I'm not going to bank the rest of it."

Instead, he leveraged his advantage of available cash by finding good deals on merchandise and buying it in quantity. That happened a lot. If it was a particularly good value, he'd buy even more and stash it in the store. Pallets of the merchandise would arrive, and he'd sell it at a very competitive price until it was gone. That made for a true win-win for John and the customer. That's how he could afford to give a box of ammunition away when he sold a gun, or threw in an extra pair of gloves with a larger purchase.

When Green Acres first opened it wasn't very big ... about the same size as your average 7-Eleven gas station outlet. Over the years it expanded six times, adding more floor space, storage, and a few offices. John did nearly all of it with cash, and as he made more he expanded more. On some slow days he used to walk around the building with shining eyes and arms waving saying, "Let's go ahead and expand here ... let's do this, or let's do that." And so it grew.

An Icon

Phillip Gazaleh said among the good business practices at Green Acres was his grandfather's true 'heart' of service for his customers. He believes that drew his first clients, and keeps them coming. The great thing about that kind of attitude is the generational benefit: the Farhat's who run the store now talk about all the descendants of original clients who continue to frequent their store. Like a family tradition of visiting Knotts Berry Farm every year, original client's sons, granddaughters, and their children, come into the store out of tradition even if it's out of their way. They're never disappointed because manners, attention to detail, and care about the customer comes through every time. They remember John and have fond memories of coming in the store as young kids. Later in adulthood they keep coming, and that keeps John's kids going as well.

If one looks around at the big sporting goods chain stores anywhere in the country, they'll find big, sleek retail outlets staffed mostly by part time high schoolers or college students trying to make a buck. While they're usually well-groomed and helpful, rarely can they dig into a product with any detail. On the other side of the spectrum lies Green Acres, with its four-generations of Farhats and their spouses who weaned on all things Green Acres. They started with hard work in the adjoining garden, and moved into the store as full-time experts on everything they sell.

Like any successful enterprise, customer service is number one. That's the credo John Farhat drove deep into the thinking of anyone who went to work there. Customer service is not just a slogan on a wall or atop a corporate report; they really live by it. That's one thing the "big box" stores cannot surmount. Unless price is the only driver motivating the customer, what comes with the personal experience of buying and maintaining outdoor equipment is the relationship with a sales representative who really knows what they're talking about. Every one of the Green Acres employees has deep experience with outdoor life, and it comes across. To the sporting or hunting enthusiast, they are like an expectant mother walking into a Babies R Us store to find all the associates eight months pregnant themselves. They've been there, are there, and know exactly what she wants.

If all a customer wants is the absolute lowest price and they don't care about intelligent, caring customer service, then they might as well shop at one of the big box stores. Having said that, Green Acres' prices are highly competitive anyway. If a customer looks around and identifies ten random items, six of them will be the same price as, or lower than, the competition. Two might be higher-priced, but then two will be lower, so it evens out. That's how they managed to stay in business all these years while some chain stores came and went.

As a side note, Green Acres also offers service for numerous products sold by the big boxes since big boxes don't have the in-house expertise to service or repair their products. K-mart and Walmart used to send their customers to Green Acres for repair work because of their expertise, since Green Acres carried the same product line. Until then, clients had to mail the product back to the manufacturer and wait for months until they get it back.

It all goes back to customer service. That was the most important thing to John, and that is part of his legacy. Again, competitors will hire sales representatives off the street, give them rudimentary training, and put them behind a counter. Green Acres staff have actually used it in the field and can testify to its value. If it's of little value, they won't have it on their shelves. If a customer asks about a brand they don't stock any longer, there's usually a reason for it. "This one gave us problems when we tried it," or, "That one worked, but was way too expensive for what it did."

In John's words: "Treat your customers like gold, because they're the reason we're here. They're the ones who put food on your table." The rest of his boiled-down advice is obvious to any visitor at their store. "Take pride in your business. Make sure it's clean and looks nice. And have a fair price."

Never a Chain

If Green Acres ever became a chain, they would lose the very thing that keeps them unique. That's because a successful family business has two ways to go: expand and lose the personal touch while gaining volume and profitability, or stay small and strong. John's business expertise could have taken him far in the chain store business. Just look around at the proliferation of sporting goods stores in the last twenty years. He had to see that, but he realized not only the personal touch would be lost, but his family would have "gone corporate" as well. It wouldn't have ended only with the loss of his close-knit family, but he would also lose the customer base who became part of his extended family. The energy that came from familiar folks walking through the door season after season became the glue that kept Green Acres local and strong.

If a customer or a member of his family was sick, or if a wedding was imminent, John mentioned it to them. No matter if it was six months later, he remembered. When someone reaches deep into another's life like that, they establish an indelible bond that lasts beyond the monetary transaction. "How's your dad doing?" "When is the graduation?" Has the reader experienced this when shopping at a hardware store? A supermarket? Anywhere? Far more than purchasing an item and leaving, a Green Acres visit is an experience more like, "We want to know how you're doing, and might have heard through the grapevine that this person has a sick family member and we haven't seen them for a while because they're going through a tough time," and so on. Or, "Hey I heard about such and such … how's she doing?" That's the soul-level dynamic John's children and grandchildren do not want to lose.

No matter how educated or visionary one of them might be, family relationships far outweigh consideration of becoming a chain. After all, how do you replicate love? You can't. It's not a cookie-cutter transaction to be outsourced to a cadre of so-called professionals armed with spreadsheets and forecasts predicting market share advances by pennies on the thousands based on fifty years of low-interest loans. Green Acres is a hybrid, a one-only kind of human-to-human profession that should not extend beyond their borders—not if they want to retain the family ethos envisioned by John Farhat. That's the golden experience they do not want to lose.

Stand-alone stores like theirs have plenty of competition. According to Z Farhat, their business is only one of two in the entire US southeast that offers the same mix of product and service.

"In Northeast Florida, Southeast Georgia, and even into South Carolina, we're the largest of our kind. There are other sporting goods stores that have more guns, but they sell guns only, and they don't carry other products like we do. And they don't offer a full line of archery products, or fishing products like we do. And they don't have the general line of hunting gear that we do. They'll just sell you a gun and some ammo and that's it."

While the big box stores offer some discounts, they don't have a full time gunsmith, archery expert, or fishing pro shop help that can service *everything* in the store. If Green Acres can service the item in the store, they'll do it. If not, they won't box it up and send it out. They'll take care of it in quick order one way or another, or replace it with a new one.

"One of our mottos," said Z, is 'If we don't have it, you don't need it.' And that's really true. We try to have a little bit of everything."

Chapter 10

Staying Flexible

Starting in the nineties when the Jaguars first came on the scene, players like Mark Brunnell and Tony Bocelli shopped Green Acres for their outdoor and hunting attire. That was also the period when Jeanette—in her spare time between cooking and taking care of children and grandchildren—handled the store's clothing line. Of course, the reason they came was for the quality and personal service. When it came to clothing, most of the box stores carried less-expensive items that faded or ripped after one or two washings. They were good for about one season. What they found at the Farhat store might have cost twice as much as the competition, but the material lasted four times as long and over several seasons. Products like GoreTex and Carhart with goose down insulation provided comfortable, durable wear. That went for boots and other hunting apparel. Jeanette made sure the carried every size from infant (serious hunters train their young at an early age) all the way to XXXL, which suited the needs of Jacksonville's new NFL breakout team. But the clothing line eventually came to an end.

There were a few reasons Green Acres ceased their line of clothing. First, the big box stores started carrying their own brand name and sold it for less than half of what Green Acres offered. That happened more and more, and over time as new generations of buyers permeated the market, their perceptions of price vs. quality blurred. Apparently, they preferred to pay less, use it a season until the material ripped at the seam and the zipper broke, and then throw it away. So it goes with new generations.

Secondly, the market isn't what it used to be. During the nineties when the US economy was in better shape, many customers took long hunting trips to far off places. When that happened they invested in more durable clothing that would last through a number of environments, knowing they wouldn't have to buy more on the other end.

The third had to do with the weather. Al Gore's doomsday prophesy aside, winters in this part of the country have moderated in recent years. It's simply not as cold as it used to be, so the need for high-quality, warm outdoor wear has dwindled. Before, they sold sub-Arctic temperature clothing—the kind one could wear in the South Pole without worrying about quality. Back then, people bought because they could afford the long trips, and it was a lot colder. Today, when a customer enters the store and looks to the right, he'll find the entire wall where the clothes used to be covered by a complete line of fishing equipment.

Collards & Food Stamps

Growing up as the second youngest son, I had everything I wanted. They gave me everything I needed, but not just me of course. That was true of the whole family. And they expected me to work, so I worked! As long as you worked, you had everything you wanted. That's all there was to it. If you didn't work, you didn't get nothin'. That's pretty much the way it is around here still. That's not going to change I don't think.

Growing up, I did a little bit of work gardening. When we first moved here when I was about ten, I had my own vegetable stand out front of the house. I grew green onions and collard greens and stuff, and sold them at the stand. It was just a couple of little tables, and I had a few regular customers. One black lady, a regular customer, had a nickname for me. She used to call me "peaches."

My dad went to the farmers market every day to pick up vegetables for his store, and he'd always get me a couple cases of peaches to put up front with my other produce to sell. That's how that black lady gave me my name. She always used to buy from me and pay me more than what we were selling them in the store for, so she must have liked me or something. She was a very sweet lady.

Dad's garden was big, and I had two rows for my stand. They were mostly green onions because they were easy to grow. Almost all the money I earned from the stand I saved, and put right in the bank. I didn't have to give a percentage to Dad, or pay him. He just let me keep it. I guess that was how I learned to run a business.

One day when I was several years older my cousin, Ray Farah, and me took a load of collard greens to the place they gave out food stamps. It was Ray's idea: he said to load the greens into my dad's old station wagon and drive over to where they gave out the food stamps. We'd sell our greens to the people who just got their stamps and we'd take them in exchange for the collard greens. We did that because they accepted stamps at the store and it was easy for them to pay. It worked out good because the people didn't think we could take food stamps, but they didn't mind giving you whatever you wanted for your greens. We cleaned up that day, and made so much money! In a way, we took our greens on the road so to speak. They would give you more because we were accepting food stamps. We cleaned up. That was the most money we ever made. So, yeah, we learned how to make money. I saw what it takes.

One day when I was around twelve I watched Dad give some guy our Pontiac Bonneville. This guy was walking to work every day and Dad thought he needed a car, so he gave him the car. He goes, "Pay me when you can." Of course, the guy never showed up again. Now we didn't have an extra car. I mean, we had a car, but the Bonneville was an extra car. I said, "Dad, he just took our car." "Yeah," he said, "he needed it worse than we did."

He probably knew he would never pay him, but that's just the way he was. He said he didn't really need the car. It was worth probably $200 or $300 bucks, not much, but that's just how big his heart was. He just gave people everything. But he always felt like it would come back somehow. And I think it did, because business has been good ever since. Every year it got better.

That's why everybody loved him. You won't find a person that will say a bad word about him. I waited all these years for somebody to say, "Hey, that son-of-a-so and so ...!" But I never heard it.

Abie Farhat

Family First

Technically, Abie Farhat, John's youngest son, wears the shoes of CEO for Green Acres. But by everyone's account including his own, Abie is more a crossing guard for the lives of his extended family in their mutually-owned business than he is a forceful boss. When it comes to decisions, they all fit in one of two baskets: little decisions and big ones. Abie makes the little decisions all the time and does not feel the need for consultation. But when it comes to the big ones he follows his father's example: he won't make a move without asking his brothers. Like his father, he'll gather the rest of his family at someone's house and casually discuss the situation over grilled steaks and beer. Eventually, the answer arrives somewhere between the second helping of potato salad and the strawberry shortcake.

Big decisions are kept within the echelons of the three brothers and never become the concern of the grandchildren. There's no rush for them since they're still on their lifelong learning curve and will someday assume the mantle of leadership. Similar to a committee, major decisions are better dealt with through fewer heads. Occasionally a situation might call for the entire staff—twelve employees—to discuss it. Such meetings would call for the opinions and perspectives of everyone, such as the layout of a display case for a new product line or the color of the refurbished back area of the store. In such cases, the meeting would take place in one of their larger homes, or over dinner at a local restaurant. In any case, since the same blood runs through all veins there's very little to get bent out of shape about. Generally speaking, everyone is on the same page anyway. But even if they're not, John's strict, loving guidance taught them to respect whoever is in charge. As of now, that's Abie. His approach has always been to gain consensus of all his brothers, and if they are not in full agreement, he won't push on with a new direction until they are.

Their family first philosophy works in the store as well as at home, as if they're interchangeable. Somehow the Farhat offspring all work together and hang out together, which is amazing when one considers the staunch individualism prevailing in this country. Sure, each of the Farhat children have others outside the family they do things with, but they also choose to do things together. As Z pointed out, "People are like, 'Man, you see these guys six days a week and then on Sunday you gotta see them again?'" Apparently yes, and that's okay too.

That's what John taught them. He did it in such a way as to prevent the usual young adult rebellion that drives kids away from home, parents, and siblings in the name of individual development. While some of that is good, the Farhat family accomplished that without all the wrenching separation found in most American homes. If we look at the statistics in Ramallah, and Middle-Eastern cultures in general, family businesses make up 85 percent of the Arab world's non-oil GDP. That's a lot compared to America, where 63 percent of the workforce are family-run businesses. And "family run" in America can mean a mega corporation with hundreds of employees while technically owned and run by a family. That's not the case in Palestine.

John's penchant for keeping the family together might have heightened when he looked around his new environment and saw American youth spread their wings, only to return occasionally for Thanksgiving, Christmas, weddings, and funerals. He was not about to let that happen. As Abie pointed out, "Regardless of what goes on in the store, we must always be close and stay together. We get away once in a while to do our own thing, but we always end up back here for sure."

John's priorities were clear: Family first and business second. Z recalled the time when an important issue came up requiring the entire family's input. As a result, half the store would have to take the day off and because it was on a Saturday, they would be overwhelmed with customers. Z approached his grandfather and suggested those who had to work should not attend the meeting. John didn't think twice about his answer. "Well, we'll just close down the store for the day." As it turned out, they worked the store with a skeleton crew supplemented by a few part-timers and got by. Then they closed down for the second half of the day.

Like any normal family, conflict happens within the Farhat clan. Sometimes in the heat of a busy day when everyone is maxed out and words are about to fly, they'll turn the customer over to someone else and take the issue to the back of the store where it's resolved. If it happens in front of one of their long-term customers, they usually laugh about it and carry on. They've seen it all before. Two seconds later, it's over anyway. Apparently there's never been a long drawn-out confrontation. Instead the scenario might be somebody who thinks they're busier than everybody else and asks for help with a customer, when in fact everybody is slammed. Normal stuff like that.

"I run the gun department," said Z, "along with my cousin, Phillip. My brother, John, works in the shop and my other cousins, Eddie and Bradley, work in the archery department. That's the thing about our business; if they need help in archery, I can go to archery. If they need help in the fishing, I can go there. We're all trained to do everything else. If someone is on vacation in archery, somebody has to cover who knows what they're doing in archery. No problem. We have five people in archery and only two people in guns, so sometimes I need to help them out, and vice versa."

Eddie Farhat, Jr. has been on the payroll as a full time employee for over thirteen years. Prior to that, he worked off and on during school and weekends for twelve years and, of course, he did a stint in John's garden picking weeds, tilling, planting, and copping a watermelon now and then. "With that kind of background none of us turned out to be too lazy," he said.

In all, twenty-five years is a big chunk of his life. Like his relatives, Eddie does a little bit of everything in the store. He helps out in the front with customers, does sales, takes care of the emails, and runs most of the electronic part of the store. He also does a little cleaning, shipping, customer service, and whatever else needs to be taken care of. With all the family members cross-trained in virtually every department, Green Acres approaches the model of a well-oiled machine with interchangeable parts.

Jamie might be one of the offspring not intimate with the rest of the departments in the store. Today she helps out in the office on the administrative side of things, including logging the guns when they come in to insure the all-important paper trail is accurate. On the other end, when a client buys a gun she'll insure they're dispensed to the customers with accurate documentation. Much of her work coincides with Abie's wife, Maysoon, who takes care of the bookkeeping for the store.

Just Do a Fair Deal

I remember we used to work with Grandfather out in the garden. He let us ride the tractor, and we use to think we were driving and controlling it. The garden was hard work. Then at the end of the week if it was in the summer, he would take us to the beach with picnic tables and we'd grill our food. Sometimes he took us to St. Augustine's historic fort, or maybe to the movies. But he wouldn't take us to anything unless it was educational. He also took us to the Museum of Science and History once, and sometimes to the public library. My parents took us places too, but my grandfather took us when my parents were busy in the store. Back then both Mom and Dad worked full-time, so Grandpa would say, "You know, I got the kids, okay?"

Like everyone else in the family, I started to work in the store when I was around 5 or 6 years old. Grandpa would stick a broom in my hand and say, "Here, go sweep the floor." Or he'd tell me to Windex the doors or the countertops. So we'd work: me, my brother, and my cousin, Philip ... all of us. If Grandpa saw us working, sometimes he would give

---

us a reward: "Hey, let's go. I'm taking you for an ice cream." Sometimes at the end of the day he'd give us a $20 bill, or take us out to eat.

Throughout middle school we would come home and go right to the store to help out. In high school I worked every Saturday for as long as I can remember. When I went to college I had classes every day but Friday, so I'd work in the store both Friday and Saturday. On other days when I got out of class at 2:00, I'd work until 6:00. If I got out at noon, I'd still work at the store until 6:00. So as a full time student I put in about 40 hours per week. After college, I went to work at the store full-time.

If someone asked me what the biggest lesson I learned from Grandpa was, I wouldn't say it was hard work. I would say he taught me to always be charitable, and trust people. If he was getting ripped off or whatever and he knew it, he'd say, "Listen … let them do it. It will come back to you tenfold." He would literally let people *take* merchandise with them and they'd say, "I'm going to pay you back." Sometimes they paid him back, and sometimes they didn't.

Grandpa was blessed with prosperity, yet he gave so much to our church—not just our church but also to other churches. He also did stuff for the homeless, set up food banks, and bought meals for the needy, especially around the holidays. He'd do a lot of other things like sell a gun for a hundred dollars below his cost—not all the time but once in a while. He'd say, "Listen, you made a sale and that's the main thing. Don't worry; it will come back to you because people will remember that."

Once, a guy came in and wanted to buy his son his first gun for Christmas. But he couldn't afford it and my grandfather knew it. So he just said, "Here, Merry Christmas. Give it to your kid." Years later, that same guy turned himself around and became a multimillionaire. He's been a big customer of ours ever since, and spends a lot of money at our store. The man's son remembers that story, and he still has that shotgun and plans to give it to his own kids.

Grandpa's philosophy was, "Don't worry about getting the better end of the deal; just do a fair deal. He was never greedy either, and he didn't like taking advantage of anybody. But there was a difference between being kind and being taken advantage of. He'd do a kind act if a situation called for it, but he wasn't going to just let people take guns for nothing.

He used to read Bible Scriptures to us a lot, especially when we were younger. And he often talked about forgiveness, which he had to exercise a lot in his life. He'd say, "Hey, just let it be," like water off his back.

There was a number one thing my grandfather used to say, and he said it right up until he passed away. In fact, we used to kind of make fun of him when he said it: "Keep the family together. If our family's going to be fractured while the store makes record profits, then close down the store!"

Z Farhat

An Administrative Nightmare

Running a sporting goods store with hunting equipment and guns requires a lot of behind-the-scenes work. Paperwork. So much more than people see from the outside. Considering the firearms alone, in today's anti-gun climate the burden of accountability is more and more on the seller, and every gun has to be strictly accounted for. If it is found that just one goes missing, the authorities can shut down the whole operation.

"That's the stressful part of the business that people don't see," said Abie. "Many of our relatives and friends alike think we're making money hand over fist, but they don't see the stressful part it. Sometimes it feels like the Bureau of Alcohol, Tobacco, and Firearms (ATF) owns the business. They have the right to take our license at any time."

Beyond the paperwork and accountability are hefty insurance premiums. Gun retailers have to pay three times the amount or more than any other business, and it goes up every year. Like the insurance companies in Florida that stopped writing policies after so many hurricanes, insurers don't want to cover gun shops because of all the negative press in recent years. Providers like State Farm or Prudential have pulled out, saying guns shops are too much of a liability, particularly with the mounting lawsuits popping up across the country against the makers—and sellers—of guns. Green Acres has to go with specialized insurance companies who charge enormous premiums for liability. According to Abie, their policy goes up a few thousand dollars every year. Recently it increased a whopping $10,000 over a two year period alone.

People are scared of getting sued, and as a result, a one-million dollar umbrella policy isn't near enough any longer. It has to be at least $10 million, which adds to the tremendous overhead required to run a successful sporting goods store. So if Green Acres or any other gun retailer makes any money, a large chunk of the profit goes to liability insurance. That brings us back to John Farhat's philosophy of reinvesting in the business instead of tucking the profits away somewhere else. In short, Green Acres is paid for. The building. The land. Their home. That means they can keep prices low and still make a profit. Abie said if they had to pay a lease on their building, they couldn't make it. "Anybody trying to start off now would need multiple millions of dollars just to get it off the ground."

When asked how the recent hype about strengthening gun laws affected their business, Abie had this to say. "Obama was the best salesman *ever* for the gun business. Prices for guns, ammunition, and everything associated with it went through the roof when Obama started talking about gun laws. Everybody made a lot of money. My dad was so happy watching us get real busy with the increase of gun sales. At one point, Hillary Clinton said she would allow people to sue the gun shops, the manufacturers, and the ranges. Fortunately, she wasn't elected. But in the meantime, folks kept stocking up on their guns while they could."

Ted Bundy

An unfortunate liability case in point happened in 1979, when John took the witness stand in the Ted Bundy trial for the murder of two coeds at the University of Florida. Apparently Bundy bought a knife from Green Acres that he intended to use in the murders, but never did. The police traced the knife back to John's business through a sales receipt found on the floor of Bundy's car.

In those days, liability wasn't the issue it is today, so no one attempted to go after John or Green Acres. In fact, one of the newspapers reported that "…it goes along with this business of selling knives and firearms. Sometimes people are going to misuse them." It was true then and it is true in the world we now live in. John testified that he recognized Bundy since he sold the knife to him, and that was that. By that time, Bundy was on his way to the electric chair anyway, so it wasn't a big deal.

Trust, or Nothing

Over his forty-six years in the business, John built up a formidable cadre of suppliers. Pick any manufacturer of guns, ammunition, archery, or anything else available in their store, and they've likely supplied Green Acres. Crossman BB guns, Bear Archery, Browning, Smith & Wesson, Remington, and Colt to name a few. The list is long, evidenced by the impressive display in the store. Years of creditworthiness let John and his sons take advantage of little or no interest on delivery payment, which also helped keep profits up and prices down. Not to mention their credit limit; suppliers never question them when placing an order because they know they'll be paid on time or before the due date. If the deadline was ninety days, John often paid in thirty. With that kind of integrity, no wonder their credit limit is, well, almost unlimited.

On time, a supplier (name omitted) became a little nervous about being paid after receiving a particularly large order from John. It was a local supplier, and because they doubted John's payment record they only shipped a portion of what he ordered. When John called and asked for thirty more guns the rep replied, "Mr. Farhat, my boss is afraid you're not going to be able to come up with the money." Without missing a beat, John asked him how much he owed the supplier, right down to the penny. The supplier said he owed them $12,432.09. John said, "Okay, I'll be in your office in about a half an hour to make the payment."

John showed up at the reps office with a grocery bag full of ones, fives, twenties, and change—whatever he had—in the exact amount of $12,432.09, and dropped it on the rep's desk. Before he could say anything, John said, "Give me a receipt. I don't want to do business with you no more. Thank you very much."

It was a local distributor who should have known about John's good reputation. As a result, John was very embarrassed knowing they thought he would default on his account. He kept his word and never did business with that supplier again.

That was another aspect of John: he kept strict control of his credit line debt. Everything was paid on time. If anybody thought he would default on his payments, it hurt him deeply. He felt if he extended trust to so many people himself, that he deserved the same kind of trust in return.

***

There is another story about trust, but the other way around. Right after John opened his new convenience store on Normandy, one of his customers from his former store on the north side showed up. The old woman happened to be one of John's detractors, and always accused him of overcharging her. When she appeared from clear across town, John wondered if her mission in life was to irritate him. She bought a bag of groceries and took it to the counter and John rang her up.

"Oh that's too much," she said, peering at him through narrowed eyes. "You must've mis-rung something Mr. Johnny."

John said okay, took everything out of the bag, and tallied it up again. When he finished and told her what she owed him, she said, "No, that's too much, you must have rung it up wrong again."

John looked at her a moment and came to a decision.

"I tell you what," said John, forcing a smile, "you take the groceries home and add it up yourself. If I'm right, you come back and pay me. And if I'm wrong, you don't owe me nothing." She said okay, then took the bag and left. Abie saw the whole thing.

"Dad," he said, "she'll never come back and pay you, even if you're right."

John smiled and said, "Oh, I know. But I just got rid of my headaches for $25, so I got off cheap."

"But how? … she'll never come back."

"That's right," he said, "and I won't ever have to worry about her again. It's worth it."

John has done that several times over the years. While it looks like he gave merchandise away when it might have been more prudent to press in and win his point, he considered trusting relationships far more important than a few lost dollars. Another example is the guy who bought a box of shells and accused John of charging too much. His response was like the one he gave the old lady: "Just take it. You can pay me for it later." The man never came back, but again John believed he came out ahead in the deal. "I know he's not coming back, but for one ten-dollar box of shells, I don't have to deal with that headache anymore."

Since word of mouth is the least expensive and most effective way to advertise, the nervous supplier and antagonistic old lady probably sent a lot of business to John's store. Although their experience was not altogether pleasant, when they talked about John Farhat, they could only have good things to say about him.

***

John's concept of fairness and integrity in the marketplace never wavered. One time a customer came to the store and wanted to sell him his gun. John was busy with another customer, so the man had to wait. In the meantime, a new customer arrived and struck up a conversation with the man waiting for John. A few minutes later the customer bought the gun from the guy, and both left the store.

Several days later the man who bought the gun came back to the store. When John saw him he slapped a Green Acres utilities bill in the man's hand. When he looked up with a curious expression, John told him he should pay it.

"What do you mean, pay it?"

"If you're going to do business in my store," said John, "you might as well help pay my overhead."

The man just stared while John continued. "That's right. I expect you to pay my electricity bill. I was going to buy that gun and you walked in and bought it out from under me. That's the rudest thing anybody could do."

"Oh, I'm sorry Mr. Johnny ... I didn't realize I did that!"

That was one customer who kept coming back.

***

When Abie was picked to run the store, he had some pretty big shoes to fill, and he admits it. "I can't really fill those shoes," he said recently. "I'm not cut out the same as my dad. I'm just different ... just too strict business-wise. They put me here to run it and I can be too hard at times because I don't want to let Dad down. I don't do it to be mean, I do it for the store. I don't mean it personally, but I lose it sometimes when it might not have been that big a deal. But it was a big deal to him, so it's big to me."

Politics and Clients

A large percentage of Jacksonville's one million-plus population is classified as "outdoor persons." Within that mix are fishermen, anglers, sportspersons, wildlife watchers, hunters, and participants in "other wildlife-related activities." A recent poll indicated there are 7.6 million Florida residents and non-residents who do outdoor activities inside Florida every year. At some point in time, every one of them will buy some kind of equipment, weapon, or accessory to enhance their sport. They find it either at the big box stores or Green Acres where quite a few of them return again and again. Because much of their business comes through positive word of mouth, several members of the entertainment, big business, and the political communities favor John's business over the others. Their patronage, coupled with John's religious and civic involvement, earned Green Acres a virtual spot on the city's Who's Who list.

Whenever a mayoral or even a gubernatorial race took place, a committee member or even the candidate, would visit John at the store to get his advice and support. Every mayor and every sheriff would call on him. He had political clout, or at least they thought he did. Another reason for their visit is John was, as usual, generous with his contributions. He also knew the judges, because a lot of them hunted. They asked John if they could post their sign along his property on Normandy boulevard, and they did. John was invited to political rallies for Delaney, Peyton, and Brown.

Before they seriously considered running for office, invariably John was contacted for advice and support. He was the man everybody liked to because he was well-liked and well-respected.

Old Ramallah Club officers – John: second from the right

Chapter 11

Equipping the Stars

Celebrities from across the country visited Green Acres. Golfer Davis
Love III who won the PGA Tour and the PGA Championship was a
regular visitor. Perry Como and his wife, Roselle often came through
the door. Bow hunter and television host Fred Bear of Bear Archery
also frequented the store. The avid hunter and singer, Ted Nugent, went
hunting with John on a couple of occasions. One year, John hunted with
famed ballet dancer Mikhail Baryshnikov who might be considered as
good with a gun as he was shooting movies or dancing. As the years
went on, the store became more famous because it was always there, and
because the Farhats ran it.

Once, when Perry and Roselle Como visited the store, Buddy's eldest
grandson, Essa, came out of the bathroom with toilet paper trailing
behind him. He was only one year old, and seeing he had a problem he
called out in a loud voice, "Mama, come wipe my butt!" Roselle Como
saw that and almost lost it. She couldn't stop laughing. According to
the story, she bought a gun that day—a Ruger .22 rifle—and went on
her way. A couple of days later she called back and she said, "I laughed
so much I forgot to give you the check. It's still in my checkbook!" She
mailed it in.

Notable CEOs and major business owners visit the store frequently
including major land owners and developers such as the former owners

of the Winn-Dixie stores, the Davis family, or the Stein family: owners of Regency Square. Included are the Barco family of Barco's Engineering, and members of the Stockton, Whatley, Davin & Company: the largest mortgage, banking, and real estate insurance firm in the US Southeast. Doubtless there were many others from across the country that came to hunt, fish, and enjoy the Florida outdoors. The word got out that a store existed in Jacksonville that had the stock, knowledge, and customer service to cater to their every need. When they stopped by, John met them with his usual laconic wit and proceeded to have fun with them. They, in turn, enjoyed John quite a bit.

Sometimes several CEOs came to the store together, and when that happened Green Acres took on the atmosphere of a middle-east marketplace. The owner of Regency Square might show up with the owner of Duval Motors or the Davis family. One of them would point to a top-of-the-line gun and say, "I'm gonna buy that one." Then another CEO might say, "I'll buy it for you." The third one might turn to John and blurt, "I'd like to buy that gun," to which John responded, "Well then, buy it." The third CEO would respond, "No, it costs too much." John's response was, "I'll let you have it for five-hundred dollars"—which sounded low-ball but fell way above his costs. Then John would coerce them to buy the gun, and he still made a handsome profit. Such as it was with some CEOs on a buying spree.

One time Tony Bocelli and Mark Brunnell came in to buy new hunting clothes. Tony's house caught fire and everything went down, including his hunting equipment, and he called ahead of time for permission to shop after the store closed. Of course John said 'yes' and when Tony and Mark arrived, several of the Farhat family was there to serve them.

Dano Davis, land owner and CEO of Winn-Dixie Stores at the time, used to shoot guns with Buddy Gazaleh. Buddy took his son, and Dano would bring his, and they'd meet at a gun club near Phillips Highway. The CEO of Blue Cross/Blue Shield also shopped at Green Acres before going on his extended pheasant hunting trip in Michigan. He shopped all kinds of stuff, and off he went. All those people received good service, and when they talked with their friends—other CEOs and such—over the campfire, they mentioned Green Acres in glowing terms. That's probably why so many kept coming and coming through the years.

A Real Extrovert

When I decided to change my major, I was amazed when both my grandfather and grandmother were okay with it. She went along the same lines as Grandfather, like whatever is gonna make me happy, she was on board with that. As far as my education went, she's more on the side of trying to figure out the match making aspect of my life. Who am I going to get married to? When am I going to have kids? That sort of thing. His side was more like what I am going to do with my life. She had input, but it was really more that she was supportive of me, and him being supportive of me. Even now, she's still trying to match make me. Oh, yeah, I would say that is her number one quality. She's kind of funny because sometimes you'll think she's not really paying attention to things, but when she gets into her matchmaking side of things she's in high gear. She knows what she's doing, like a professional.

The urging I got from my grandfather to shoot high in education seems to be a thing aimed mostly at the women in the Farhat family. My aunt Cindy said the same thing. "Auntie, did you get the same kind of pressure?" I asked. "Oh, yeah," she answered. "I'm not really sure why that is. If I would get a B in school or an A ... not quite an A+, he goes,

"You're slacking!" It was a joke of course, but he still said it. Or if I said I got a 100 on my test, he'd go "Just 100?"

I think he just wanted us to succeed, to have the opportunities maybe he didn't have growing up. I think he wanted it for the men, too, but they had a sense that they needed to continue what he started with the family business. They feel more drawn to keep this going. It's probably a cultural thing too, because once you get married, as a woman you become part of the male's family. With the guys, when they get married they can bring their wives into the business here too, if that's what they want to do."

About my grandfather, he's the definition of an extrovert, like very 'out there.' He just loved being around people, loved socializing with people. That was one of the things I think that made his business so great, that he was so inviting with the customers, and welcoming. He made everybody feel like family. That was something he did with all of us too. With so many grandkids, so many family members, he made everybody feel like they were his favorite. He had a good knack of talking with people the right way, and listening too.

Jamie Farhat

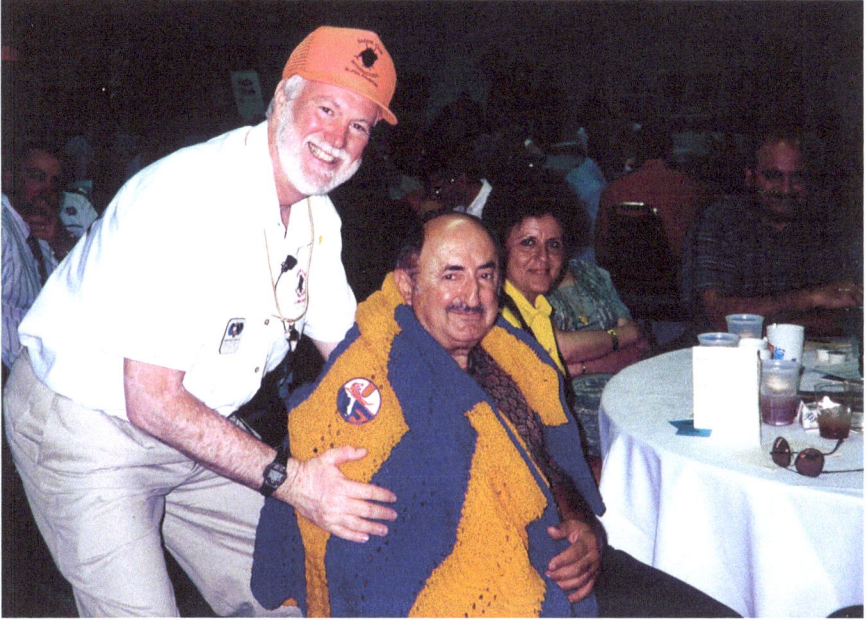

Florida State fan! – mid-90s

Chapter 12

The Church

Like all Ramallah immigrants, from day one John Farhat's DNA was infused with the teachings of the Orthodox Christian Church. Insuring he would hold on to his roots and impart his faith to his family, he never wavered from his participation in the church. Until his last days, John placed much of his heart and worldly gain in his local Antiochian body. In addition to raising their children, work at Green Acres, and other endeavors, both he and Jeanette sowed into their church and other Christian oriented works around Northeast Florida.

Since most people outside of the Ramallah community are not aware of the Farhat's spiritual roots, a brief history will help.

The Antiochian Orthodox Christian Archdiocese of North America dates back to the earliest days of Christianity when followers of Jesus Christ were first called, "Christians." That story is found in the Bible, in the eleventh chapter of the book of Acts. It was also the place where the Apostle Paul of Tarsus, with Barnabas, set out on their great missionary journey to the non-Jewish world—a tradition that would last for centuries up to this day. Those early Christians planted churches throughout Syria, Asia Minor, the Caucasus Mountains, Mesopotamia, Greece, The Balkans, Italy and most of the Mediterranean region. It is from those original missionaries that today's Antiochian Church got its name.

As previously explained, in the late eighteen-hundreds events in the homeland forced Antiochian Christians to emigrate to other parts of the world. Later in the mid-nineteen-hundreds, more Antiochian Christians, notably from Ramallah, continued to leave. The spiritual needs of those who settled in North America were first met through the Russian Orthodox Church or the Greek Orthodox Church, which had been established in the USA since the late seventeen hundreds. After the turn of the century however, the First World War and the Russian Bolshevik Revolution brought ruin to the Orthodox churches in much of the world, including North America. After these crises, some orthodox communities became loyal to the Russian Church while others were loyal to the Patriarchate of Antioch. That was solved in 1975, when the Metropolitan of the Antiochian Archdiocese of New York and the Metropolitan of the Antiochian Archdiocese of Toledo, signed what was known as the "Articles of Reunification." Since then, there has been unity among all Antiochian Orthodox Christians.

Today there are over four hundred Antiochian clergy in 266 churches and missions throughout the United States and Canada. But when John Farhat built his new home and business on the West Side, there was no such church in Jacksonville. That would soon change.

***

When the Farhats lived on the north side, they occasionally attended a local Greek Orthodox Church. If the family couldn't make it there, a kind lady picked up the four children and took them to an Assembly of God church Sunday school while Jeanette made lunch and John worked the store until noon. John felt he should open on a Sunday for a few hours because very few people in their community owned cars and couldn't go to a larger store. He opened in the morning so they could buy their necessities and then closed mid-day (back then, Orthodox and other Christians felt Sunday was a holy day and no one worked unless they had to). When they moved to the west side on Normandy, they attended the little Baptist Church next to their house.

When it came to exposure to religion, John insured his children went to some church, as long as it was Christian and as long as they attended every Sunday. By the time they arrived at their new home on the west side, and after John and a few others helped establish the St. George Antiochian Church in Jacksonville, the kids had been exposed to three

With Eddie at the old church – 1978

Christian churches: Assembly of God, Greek Orthodox, and Baptist. Not one of them said they were confused by that, rather the consensus is they all benefitted from the diverse approaches to the church while deepening their faith.

Of course not all of them went willingly. Third son Jack Farhat said they went to church regularly with the help of a bribe now and then. "Being kids," he said, "we didn't always want to go, so my parents would say, 'Hey listen: you go to church and when you get out we'll take you over to Mr. D's Restaurant.' That always worked because Mr. D's served a big double sirloin steak, and since I was a big eater back then, I was in."

Jack said the church was definitely a big part of their upbringing and helped them learn much about morality. "Of course we learned from our parents as well, but mostly by their example. But for Dad, it was a very important, big deal to him."

He Said What Was On His Mind

I first met John Farhat when I was the lead architect for the St. George Antiochian church on Bowden road. When I started, they'd just purchased the land. John was on the building committee and he was one of the first people I met for the project. He had a sincere interest in the physical environment of the property since he had a love for trees. Over time, we got to know each other well. I found he loved the outdoors, gardening, and nature in general.

John was always sort of a big brother to me. He always tried to help and was very supportive of my designs and efforts. He was very accommodating and very enterprising ... a true entrepreneur and pioneer. Thanks to his successful store on Normandy. John was able to contribute a lot of money to the church.

I vividly remember early on when he invited me over to his store. He gave me a fig tree from Syria, and I still have it in my back yard. It makes the largest figs I've ever seen. He also gave me sweets they kept on hand at his house. I got to know his wife and eventually John and I became good friends. He was a very busy man and had a lot of things going on. He was also a serious person, but always put a little bit of humor in his life and conversation.

I guess as an architect of many years and being involved with a lot of churches and building committees, there are a few real champions that emerge in the process. John was one of them. He stood up and said what was on his mind, and then did what he believed in. But he did it without arrogance or pride ... he just made things happen. I never saw so many people at a memorial service as the one for John Farhat.

Ted Pappas, a Longtime Friend

St. John's Antiochian Church

According to Father Kamal Al-Rahil, current pastor of the St. George Antiochian Orthodox Church of Jacksonville, John Farhat always wanted to attend a church of the same denomination, culture, and tradition as their church in Ramallah. While the other churches served the purpose of proving spiritual teaching and atmosphere, it fell short of what he knew was best. He wanted his children to grow up in an *Antiochian* church—the real thing. He eventually realized his dream.

In 1973, a Jacksonville resident named Sam Newey, along with his family, attended a church conference in Michigan where they met the Metropolitan (essentially the Bishop) of the Antiochian Church of North America. While there, Sam's daughter, Pam Newey, asked the Metropolitan about a church in Jacksonville. Father Al-Rahil said she asked him straight out:

"*Sayedna*—Your Eminence, we would like to have a church in Jacksonville."

After some further discussion, the Metropolitan sent two seminarians to explore the city to see if there was enough of a base to start the church. They deemed the city very capable of supporting a new congregation, so that same year he gave them permission to start the work. From that time on, Sam Newey and John Farhat were instrumental in rallying the support to establish their church. John and Sam also helped formulate the constitution, which was incorporated in 1974. He, along with others in the city, also provided funds to get it started.

The Parish Council at the time had 12 people, and to support other parts of the work about 50 families participated. In 1974, the church was incorporated. They originally rented another church for a year and held worship services there, led by a priest from Ramallah. A year later they built their own church for their growing congregation. They remained until 1996 when they bought the property and built their existing church on Bowden Road.

***

Father Al-Rahil met John in 2001 when John was on the parish council. He said John was the first one to introduce himself.

"When I arrived, he taught me from his mind and his soul," said Al-Rahil—himself a Syrian—"the mechanisms of the church and the ethos of how things were. It was very helpful to know the people and the systems of the congregation. That was significant since 85% of the members came from Ramallah. John gave me instructions, and a book, about their culture and ways."

By then the church was established and had grown significantly. When asked what kind of a person John was, Father Al-Rahil smiled and recited what amounted to the points he covered at John's memorial service.

"He was incredible, unexpected, emotional, a fighter who can raise mountains with his determination, tenderhearted, purposeful, effective, and never afraid of work. Above all, he was very generous. Anything that was given to him, he made happen … as long as he is convinced of the need of the project. And if he believed in something, he gave it his whole mind and heart. In other words, his actions spoke louder than his words."

Aside from his regular attendance and overall financial support, John contributed a lot to the youth and its programs. He also involved the youth when feeding the homeless in downtown Jacksonville. They went at least once per month they took a complete cooked meal and passed it out to the hungry. Then on rare days when John wasn't busy with his store, garden, ministry, board meetings, and rearing his children and grandchildren, he invited father Al-Rahil and his family to his home for lunch or dinner. Father Al-Rahil estimates there are 300 families in the church today.

As a footnote: two of John's closest friends were Sam Newey, who seems to own half of Jacksonville, and Angelo Cavallaro whom he also met through the church. Sam was about nine years older than John, and Angelo was the same age. Angelo owned Cavalier Products, which he later sold to Danka Industries.

They Talked a Lot about Guns

I met John Farhat twenty-eight years ago when my wife and daughter were in West Virginia visiting another Antiochian church there. The Metropolitan of the Church was present and my daughter asked him why there was no Antiochian church in Jacksonville since there were lots of immigrants from Ramallah. The next thing, a priest named Father Harve called

---

me from San Diego and asked if I could help start a church in Jacksonville. I said I could.

The father came and met with a few of us, including John, and we decided to rent a place for a church on a temporary basis. Later they located a property on Bowden road and decided to buy it. The people in the congregation held a fundraiser and got over a million dollars, which was enough to get the church land bought and start construction. Most of the members were from Ramallah, so they identified strongly with the others in the congregation. That was around thirty years ago, and today the church is down the block from the Ramallah Club.

John got involved from the very beginning. I first met him when we were on the church council negotiating the plans for the construction. John and I were both on the committee, and later we socialized together.

On one occasion in Phoenix, I introduced John to the famous Sheriff Joe Arpaio—the one always in the news about border issues. The three of us went golfing, and John and Joe became good friends, mostly because they talked a lot about guns. I also came to help John with his real estate holdings, including the acreage behind his business and property he wanted to develop. He'd planned to build homes behind the store, but the economy changed, so decided to hold off.

Sam Newey, a Longtime Friend

Order of St. Ignatius

The Antiochian Church in North America and Canada continues to grow. With that growth came the need for greater support for its expanding programs. In January of 1975, the Metropolitan of the Antiochian Church saw the need to facilitate increased giving on the part of the laity. Until then, the church relied on voluntary donations from attendees and other sources, but it wasn't enough. The Metropolitan appointed a committee of seven trusted priests and lay people who crafted a separate organization under the auspices of the church to spearhead consistent gift giving on a broad basis. In 1976, the Order of St. Ignatius of Antioch was formally introduced.

The Order became known as the philanthropic arm of the Archdiocese, an organization of men and women who commit to give a certain amount the church on a regular basis. They came from all ages and all walks of life: factory workers, CEOs, housewives, tradesmen, business owners. It was called a "spiritual movement manifested through financial giving." Since its inception, the Order has generated around $1.4 million each year, contributing to the Antiochian programs such as missions, camp scholarships, married seminarian assistance, retired clergy, Christian education, etc. Lay people contribute to the Order through one of three levels on an annual basis: $500, $1,000, and $15,000. Those who commit to the latter are called Life Members. To date, there are around 4,000 members of the Order in North America, and John and Jeanette became Life Members early on.

The Farhat's involvement in the ministry did not end with the Order of St. Ignatius however. Jeanette recalled the many times she and John went downtown to feed the homeless.

"You know, I was working hard with the kids of course, but he often said we should feed the homeless. So I would get up in the morning and make big pots of rice and some kind of meat. For Thanksgiving, I went out and bought turkeys and took them to Woody's Barbecue to have them smoked. I used to go with John too ... but I didn't like it myself, to do all that. It was too much on me, and my knee bothered me. But I did it for him because he wants to do it. I did what he wanted me to do and I enjoyed doing it with him."

When John and Jeanette fed the homeless, they often took a group of people—kids, grandkids, members of church, and anyone else available—and served with them on the food lines.

"We always felt very good after doing that," said Jeanette. "We collected clothing from all over and donated it to the shelter. John used to go to the Salvation Army and Goodwill where he would buy clothing and take it downtown to the shelters. When it was cold, he handed out blankets. All of that."

They kept it up through thick and thin, all the way up to four years ago when John just didn't have enough energy to continue. To compensate for what he couldn't do physically, he increased his giving to the church and other organizations.

"He did it from his faith," said Jeanette, "from his heart."

Jamie Farhat, the youngest of the three children born to Eddie Farhat, said her grandfather always had good advice and was always generous. "He actually started a foundation to feed the homeless and used his own money to help the community out. It was called the Ziadeh and Jeanette Farhat Foundation, and it functioned for a long time. It later on it dissolved when Grandpa got sick."

The couple donated to local missions around the city and beyond. Wherever there was a need and John heard about it, he responded if he could. Even after he passed, Jeanette has continued to donate whenever she can. Although the foundation is no longer functioning, on a personal note she wanted to keep going, mostly because John would want it that way. She continued in the same generous spirit as her husband.

50th anniversary at the Omni Hotel, Jacksonville

Alaska cruise

Chapter 13

The Trial

On a cold January day in 1996, the Farhat family received news that would shatter their lives for years to come. John's youngest son, Eddie, had been shot in his own home.

His wife, Ghada Farhat, reportedly came home with their three children from a local gymnasium and found him on the floor bleeding profusely. He'd been shot, and the police quickly determined it was attempted murder. Ghada was arrested. Buddy, John's son-in-law, recalled the moment he heard the news.

"I was in Las Vegas at the time and I received a call from my daughter. 'Dad, when are you coming home?' I said I'd be home in a few days and we hung up. A few minutes later, she called again. 'Dad, when will you be home?' When I asked her what was going on, she said, 'Eddie was shot.' At the time I didn't relate that to my brother-in-law, because I had a cousin named Eddie and he was a somewhat *shady* character. A little later I found out that it was my wife's brother and I immediately made arrangements to fly back.

Meanwhile, Buddy's wife, Cindy, also got the call. They lived only a couple of blocks away from Eddie, so she immediately ran to their house. Eddie's body was still on the floor and the police had just arrived and wouldn't let her inside. Eddie's wife, Ghada Farhat, was in front of the house beating her hands on the grass and shouting Eddie's name. Cindy waited until they put Eddie in the ambulance, but when she tried to get inside to go with him they wouldn't let her. Ghada just sat on the ground, not paying attention.

After the ambulance left, Ghada went to the house to get her pocketbook and car keys so she could drive to the hospital. But the police said the house was off limits until they conducted their investigation. It turned out she wanted to get to the car where she hid the murder weapon. She found another ride to the Orange Park Hospital, but shortly after she arrived Eddie passed away. Then they notified John Farhat and the rest of the family.

As horrified as the adult Farhats were with the incident, Eddie's three children bore the brunt of it. They'd arrived from the gym with their mother that evening to find their father on the hallway floor. Eddie Farhat, Jr. testified later that as soon as they entered the house and found their father, his mother, Ghada, leaned over Eddie's body, grabbed the .45, and took it out to her car.

Three months later in Ghada's murder trial, the children testified that their mother tried to hide the evidence.

GREEN COVE SPRINGS
Feb. 13, 1997

Videotaped interviews with Ghada Farhat's children are expected to be introduced by prosecutors today in the Orange Park woman's trial in the 1996 shooting death of her husband. The children's testimony will state that their mother tried to hide key evidence—mainly empty .45-caliber shell casings—the night their father was slain in their home on Jan. 22, 1996, Assistant State Attorney Timothy Collins told jurors Tuesday. The children -- then ages 4, 6 and 7 -- found their father's body on

the bloodied hallway of their Marcia Drive residence
just before 8 p.m. when they returned with their
mother from 'Q'—the Sports Club on Wells Road

Eddie and his family were members of a health club on Wells Road in Orange Park. Sometime before Eddie got off work, Ghada called him and said she would take their children to the health club. She said she left his clothes in the hallway of their house, and when he got home he could pick up his gym clothes there and change.

As the story went, Ghada took their three kids to the spa, deposited them in the child care area, got back in her car, and drove home where she hid in the bathroom. When Eddie came home to get his clothes, she came out of the bathroom and shot him with a .45 pistol. Then she shot him again. And again. He fell down in the hallway and she walked over to him and shot him a couple more times, just to be sure. Then she placed the gun in her pocketbook and put it in the car. Then she returned to the spa to pick up her kids. When her children came out, one of them said, "Mama, when we came, the car was over there. So how come the car is over here?" They didn't realize that she left, and had revealed her big mistake.

After the initial shock, Ghada told the kids to sit in the front room while she called the police. It was then she took the shells and put them in a drawer in the bedroom. Next, she told the kids to run next door and tell them their father had been shot. That's when the whole family heard about the incident.

Buddy got back in town the next day and heard the news. Then John called him and asked him to take Ghada to the Sheriff's Office in Orange Park because they wanted to "talk with her." They took a long time with Ghada, so Buddy waited for them to finish. Then John arrived, and the two of them were summoned into the detective's office. He sat them both down, looked long and hard at John, and said, "There's only one person, and one person only who killed your son, and that was his wife."

They couldn't believe it. 'Ya'll are crazy," they said. "You're *crazy!*"

Nevertheless, the State Attorney told John that he could take her home with the condition that if he called him for any reason he would have to bring her back in. John said he would, and asked Buddy to take her home. Ghada stayed at Buddy and Cindy's home right up until the funeral. Her three children alternately stayed with John and Jeanette or Buddy and Cindy. One can only imagine the intense pressure felt by every one of those family members.

Like the Farhats, Ghada also came from Ramallah and was therefore part of the clan. As everyone will testify, what happened to Eddie never happens in the Ramallah community. They are too close-knit, too *accountable* for horrendous things like that to take place. The signs were there however. Sometimes Eddie left his house to go to work early in the morning, but instead of going to the store he'd walk into his parents' house and just sit in the front room. When they asked him what was the matter he wouldn't say anything. It was obvious there were some serious problems in his family, but he didn't want to talk about it.

Nevertheless, there were signs that not all was well on Ghada's side of the family either. She'd depleted her and her husband's 401-K account and IRA without Eddie's knowledge. Eddie was the computer guy in the Green Acres store, and he taught the other Farhat employees how to work the system. One of John's granddaughters worked side-by-side with Eddie and she would later testify that she knew Ghada had forged checks in Eddie's name. Ghada even stole from the business, and borrowed $10,000 the day before Eddie was killed. She just went to the bank and forged his name. These things had been going on for quite some time.

Eventually the prosecuting attorney compiled more and more evidence against Ghada, and the case went to trial. When that happened, Ghada asked John for some money so she could hire good attorneys. Since John still believed in his daughter-in-law's innocence, he loaned her $30,000 against the equity in her house so she could hire competent attorneys. After all, Ghada was a member of their Ramallah community, and therefore related to the Farhats. Her father was a Farhat, and John was a Farhat … first cousins. That's how close she was to the rest of them. So John loaned her the money because he couldn't believe she would do such a thing. It might be said that John's innate trust for others kept him somewhat blinded to the truth, at least in that case.

With that money, Ghada hired a firm called Kurtz and Block, and apparently they did a magnificent job. On the other hand the state's prosecuting attorney was nowhere near the capability to meet the challenge of her attorneys. Even though there was ample evidence to put her in jail for life, the prosecutor could not overcome the professionalism of the opposition. One example is the murder weapon. The defense attorney said the "… poor little girl (Ghada) could never shoot a .45 because it was a heavy, powerful gun, etc., etc." They listened and the defense attorney didn't' have a thing to say in response. Later they told their attorney that Ghada learned to shoot a .300 Weatherby Magnum, and also went hunting on occasion … which came naturally since she married into a family of hunters and sporting goods professionals. Nevertheless, the prosecuting attorney said he didn't need to use that information in the courtroom!

Another example was how they handled family members when it came to the witness stand. Buddy recalled his own experience.

"Since I was going to be a witness, they said I couldn't listen to the trial so I missed most of the proceedings. Then the defense attorney called me to the stand and had me state my name, which I did. Then he asked me if I knew Ghada Farhat. I said I did. Then he asked me, 'Did you know her to be a good mother?' I said I did, and that was it. I expected to be asked a lot more, but that's all they asked, and obviously that's all they wanted. The real problem came when the prosecutor failed to bring any of us to the stand to give our opinion of what kind of mother she was lately—things we said during the depositions.

The local news reported the trial was the southeastern U.S. equivalent of the O.J. Simpson trial winding down on the west coast at the time. And like the O.J. trial, the defense attorneys hired by Ghada outperformed the prosecuting attorney by miles. According to family sources the trial was as lopsided as it could get without falling over. The outcome tore the hearts of the entire Farhat family. As the papers reported at the end of the proceedings:

Ghada Farhat walked out of the Clay County Jail a free woman early yesterday after a jury found her not guilty of first-degree murder in the shooting death of her husband nearly 13 months ago.

The 30-year-old Orange Park woman flashed a broad smile as she savored her renewed freedom. But relatives of her deceased husband, "Eddie" Farhat, were reeling from the verdict.

"I don't understand it," John Farhat, the victim's father, said yesterday afternoon from his Normandy Boulevard home. "I don't want to judge. But such a justice system does not work."

Ghada Farhat emerged from the jail in Green Cove Springs where she had been incarcerated since Jan. 26, 1996 --four days after her husband was shot four times with a .45-caliber pistol in the couple's home in the Montclair subdivision of Orange Park. "I'm free finally." She said to reporters. "This is the first time I've had real fresh air in a long time." She said it also has been a long time since she held her three children, who were placed in the temporary custody of their paternal grandparents under a court order when their mother was arrested.

"I haven't seen them [children] in a year," she said. "My next step is definitely to try to get my kids back." But John Farhat said he may file a civil suit to prevent his former daughter-in-law from regaining custody. "I'm not for revenge," he said. "The main point of this story is the kids. I worry about the grandchildren. They don't want to go back to her. They're scared of her."

Another sad footnote to the tragedy occurred when reporter Robin Gouling from Jacksonville's Channel Four News asked Ghada a question when she emerged from the courthouse. "What do you have to say to your husband's parents?" Ghada laughed and responded, "They just need to get over it."

Now the focus now was on the children. Who would take care of them? John was adamant that his grandchildren, Jamie, Eddie Jr., and Bradley, should never come under the care of their mother ... ever. John took her to court knowing that since she'd been found "not guilty," that it would be tough to take kids away from their mother. Courts almost always judged in favor of the mother regardless of the situation. As soon as the suit was filed, Ghada responded in a way that was not surprising. As the news reported:

JUDGE'S REMOVAL REQUESTED

Ghada Farhat, who was acquitted of killing her husband but still faces another trial for custody of her children, charged yesterday that the judge is biased against her and asked for her removal from the case. In a motion to disqualify, Farhat said Duval County Judge Jean Johnson "has manifested an attitude and made comments and engaged in conduct . . . that indicates the judge's inability to serve fairly and impartially in this case." Farhat was acquitted in February of the January 1996 killing of her husband, Farhat Z. "Eddie" Farhat. Since her arrest, her in-laws have had custody of the children, and they are fighting to maintain custody. The custody trial is scheduled for next month.

At least some good fortune was on the side of John Farhat. Right after the trial, the lead detective (the one who said he knew who Eddie's killer was) gave Buddy Gazaleh a package, saying, "Y'all might need this later on." Inside were several letters written by Ghada while she was in jail before her trial. Without going into detail, the letters were filled with disgusting innuendo about her sexual activities in prison. They were also full of foul language and other information that left no doubt as to her incapacity to be a worthy mother of her children. What is amazing is she had no idea her letters would be intercepted while in prison. Just another indication of how naïve she was in thinking she could cover up her crime. Armed with those letters, John's lawyer presented them to the judge near the end of the hearing. He said, "Your honor, before you make your decision, we want you to read these." That did the trick. The children were assigned to the care of John and Jeanette Farhat. The tragedy of their loss of one son had been replaced by two more sons and a daughter.

***

Ghada is reported to be living in North or South Carolina, and has been arrested several times on various charges. On many occasions she tried to get a hold of the kids, but the kids refuse to talk to her. They want nothing to do with her because they know she killed their father and got away with it.

Chapter 14

The Aftermath

Throughout the ordeal, John never broke down in front of the family. Nor did he show any negative emotions. When he got the news, he simply got on the phone with his relatives and calmly said, "I want to inform you that my son, Eddie passed away." John took the entire episode and internalized it, which must have been an enormous burden. He placed his own emotions aside and conducted himself like the strong patriarch that he was. He had to lead from the very beginning, and it would turn out to be a very long road, with forgiveness as a major component. If John broke down, who would take care of things? In fact, he handled everything like a military commander.

When it became apparent what happened, naturally his sons were upset and ready to do something in response. But John told them they would do nothing; that they would all abide by the law. Buddy said, "It amazed me. His wife broke down … everybody broke down, but he did not. Eddie was his youngest son and therefore the closest to his Daddy. He was John's pride and joy, and for him to show that kind of strength after losing his favorite buddy was unimaginable."

John's mother, Sara Hanna, was far more open with her feelings. "Go ahead, invite her (Ghada) over," she said. "I want to see her … I'll grab her and I'll bust her head in!" That, from Eddie's great-grandmother who was around 90 at the time. Such was the sentiment pulsing through the family. John was the one who had to keep a sensible calm, to display a certain righteousness throughout his extended family.

Ghada remained in jail for the duration of the trial, and John never forbade the kids from visiting, or receiving calls from her. She would call the house collect, and when she did he allowed his grandchildren to talk to their mother. Even after the trial when he was granted custody of her children, he still did not deprive them. As they grew older (and the truth of what happened became crystal clear) they didn't want to talk to her anymore. John always said it was up to the kids if they wanted to speak to her or not.

"We never found out why she did it," said Buddy. "We don't know if it was the drugs or not, but she was on drugs for some time. She got thinner and thinner and it was obvious something wasn't quite right." He shook his head. "I was very close to her, and I remember her as a little kid and I was very close to her. All we could think was it was the drugs that made her take all the assets from her husband."

that it had itsJack Farhat was 36 years old at the time, and had already been married six years. "Of course it was a huge event in my life," he said. "My mom and dad already raised five of us, and then they had to start all over again with my brother's kids. Under the circumstances, it was a very bad situation, but Mom and Dad did a great job with them."

Eddie Farhat, Jr. was seven years old when his father died. He remembers when he and his siblings moved in with John and Jeanette. "It was just kind of odd, moving to a different place living with different people, so it took me a little while to warm up to them. After the first year or so I finally got in a kind of comfort zone. They let us have fun, but they were still kind of strict, making us do our schoolwork and getting our chores done. But they let us have our free time up until I was around twelve. Then it was 'go to the store, cleanup, help out, do your share.'"

Eddie recalls how they taught him the practical thing of life when he was young. "They did everything parents would do. They looked out for me, made sure I took a shower, brushed my teeth, and did my homework. They just stepped right in where my parents left off. At first it was a little weird because they were a lot more 'old-school' and traditional than my uncles and my parents were, so it was a big change. But I got used to it after a while."

When it came to being sure Eddie had enough to eat, Jeanette sometimes resorted to the old Ramallah method referred to earlier. "She would get me in a headlock and push food into my mouth. It wasn't a forced kind of thing, just the old country way of getting kids to grow up healthy. She related to a time when families cooked a lot of food and there was a lot to eat, so she did it in a loving way. When I graduated high school I weighed around 280 pounds, but then I lost about 85 pounds, so now I'm a little bit better."

According to Eddie there were no real repercussions one would expect from such a traumatic event, aside from feeling uncomfortable at first. His brother, Bradley, works full time at the store and his sister, Jamie, works there part time. So they're all still together.

"We raised two families," said Jeanette. "First we had my family with five kids; and then I raised Eddie's kids—three beautiful kids! It's been about 20 years since my son died, but we did get his children. I thank God for my husband because he's the one who saved those kids. I was too weak to think about what I wanted to do with them. They would have been with their mother and wound up on dope or something worse. Two of them work in the store and the daughter, Jamie, she's working here sometimes. I wish John could see that too, because he got very attached to that girl. He loved her to death."

"Eddie was one of my best kids in the store," she continued. "He was a very, very nice guy. He was only 30 years old. When he was killed, it almost killed my husband and me. If it wasn't for his kids coming to live with us, I don't know what would have happened. It was very tough to go through those years. Very tough. But we raised them right. They are well behaved, and honest. They followed their granddad's steps and they often say, 'We don't know any other way than the way he taught us.'"

Considering the horror of what took place in their young lives, Eddie's children could have suffered for many years, the repercussions only coming out later in their adult lives. But that has not happened. It can be said that the immediate acceptance and care given by their grandparents, prevented them from the worst case scenarios. Since Jamie spent two years in Colorado, her perspective is slightly more objective.

"It was something I had to deal with personally," said Jamie. "We all did. But my grandparents, being open and talking about things, helped a lot. We talked at least once a week or so … not that we planned it out or anything, but they would ask us how things were going. The conversation just came up, and they wanted to make sure that we knew that whatever we wanted to do, we could do. If we wanted to talk, we could. They loved us no matter what, and were very supportive."

When it came to forgiveness, John made sure the whole family knew his position. He said, "I forgive … there's no sense in not forgiving because it's not going do any good." That's one of the first things he said after everything began to settle down. "I forgive," he said. And he did.

Sarah Farhat and John – 2005

Chapter 15

The Children

John Farhat modeled some of the best characteristics for his children, insuring they would grow up to be responsible, secure, honest, and hard-working. The way he cared for others within his family, and for so many outside as well, demonstrated the highest values. Each of his children have gleaned those life lessons and incorporated them into their own lives. And it has been passed on to their children as well. Just drop by Green Acres Sporting Goods store any time of the day, and one can see John's legacy in action. There is a calm demeanor in the way the Green Acres ship is run. However, kids being kids, there were occasional periods of turmoil … particularly when it came to getting along with his siblings. Johnny Farhat laughed when he recalled one of the times.

"Oh yeah, we all got along *pretty* good, except when we got into fights growing up, like when Jack and I got in a little scuffle. We were visiting my mom's sisters up in Detroit, Michigan, and we had a game of basketball. Things got a little out of hand and we took the argument too far. The scuffle turned into a real fistfight and my mom had to come out and break it up. I immediately felt so sorry for her. Dad was back home working, and she called him up and he got on the phone. You know, my dad was firm and we knew it. When he got on the phone and told us, 'Hey cut it out right now,' we knew that was that. That's all he had to say because he was the law. He could just look at you a certain way and you knew you had to straighten up. When I had my own kids, I tried to do the same with them. I guess it worked but I still wish I was as good as he was."

Like any transplanted culture, the best things tend to remain for generation after generation. That is certainly true of the Ramallah society that grew and refined over hundreds of years. John's way of leading his family was observed by his children, and they in turn hope to pass it on to their own children. When asked if the Ramallah culture remains in his own life, Johnny said, "Hopefully it is. I want it to continue and I hope my kids will continue with it. You know, every generation here loses a little bit more of it and it seems like I'm not as involved with the community as much as my dad or mom was. And now, my kids are nowhere even close to where I am with the community, so I don't know if this will continue. But as far as I'm concerned, if I had a choice of how I would be raised, I wouldn't pick any other way. I've had a good life."

He Treated Us like Best Friends

The first thing in the morning when my grandfather came into the store, he'd laugh and ask you how you and your children were doing. Then he'd joke around with us for a while.

For Grandfather, no matter what happened, family came first. He made that most evident by taking in his son Eddie's three children into his own home after he died. He made sure they had a good house to live in, that they were taken care of and treated like any other child. Providing for everybody in the family and his extended family was his biggest goal. And for him, it wasn't about how much money he could make, but how much he could make everybody's life better.

If you talk with anyone you'll find out a common theme of his was being faithful to God. On Thanksgivings he gave away turkeys and whole dinners to soup kitchens. He made numerous contributions to charities … charities he started, and foundations he gave to. He also donated to the church, and helped build the Antiochian church in Jacksonville. He would contribute as much as he could of his time, money, and resources.

The greatest lesson I learned from him was his love for his family. He made sure that everybody was treated individually, and he had a special relationship with everybody—even to the last day. He once told me, "I always tried to treat you like best friends, not like grandchildren or children.

As we got older he'd give us our own responsibilities. He never hung over us saying, "You have to do it this way or that way." He allowed us to make our own decisions. He was stern though, and had an iron fist you know. If he wanted something done, he was going to get it done. It would usually be his way, but it not all the time. But you knew when he said something it needed to be done, whether it was to change a tractor tire or haul out the garbage.

Phillip Gazaleh

Sale! Only $6.99 (plus tax)

I worked at Green Acres when it was still a grocery store. I worked there after school and on weekends until I was nineteen. I did everything ... whatever was needed. Stocking shelves, placing orders, cleaning, or working in the garden of course. I was a jack of all trades.

My mother worked there too, and growing up it sometimes felt like she was my sister instead of my mother. We spent every weekend out there, and the entire summer working for John's mother, Sarah. Sometimes for fun we played on go-carts, chased the chickens, shot guns, or fished in the landfill behind the house that turned into a pond. Before they were married I hung out a lot with my uncles, or played basketball.

When it came to my grandfather and grandmother, I was very close to both of them. I called them Sedo and Tata: Mom and Dad in Arabic. Thirty-nine years later I still call them that, because that's what they've been to all of us: Mom and Dad.

Dad could be very funny at times. Once, we were doing inventory at the store and Dad got frustrated with the work. My little cousin was up in the attic playing around, and after a while he came down with Christmas tinsel wrapped around his head and draped down his body. He kept bugging Dad until he said, "Why don't you go out and find a tree and hang yourself on it!" The little boy didn't know what to do. It was hilarious.

Anytime I introduced Dad to anyone, be it a friend or even a customer in the store, he would always smile and tell them: "You know this is my oldest grandchild, and when he was only six days old I would put him in a basket on the counter with a price tag and try to sell him for $6.99 plus tax. But nobody wanted him." Well, instead, my mom would sit there and feed me cantaloupe all day. It's a memory I can't really remember, but hearing it a hundred times makes it seem like yesterday. I would give anything to hear Dad tell that story one more time.

Dad always expected the best from all his kids and grandkids but especially my cousin, Ziadeh and me. I'm not sure what it was, but we seemed to get singled out quite a bit when anything bad happened. While I was in Gainesville in college, I would call to check in on Mom and Dad, and as soon as I would say hello, he starts ripping into me. I asked him what was wrong, and he might tell me some of my younger cousins got into some trouble, and then he blamed me for it. So I knew no matter where we were in the world, he expected all of us to stay together and look after each other.

One thing I know all of my cousins remember is waking up at dawn to the roosters crowing and getting out in the garden. We picked whatever Tata and Sarah told us to, be it okra, onions, corn, or to jump knee deep in the mud to dig up watermelon. All the while Dad would ride his red tractor back and forth working the land. Oh, and we couldn't forget to feed the ostriches.

Essa Gazaleh

Trinity

Trinity Christian Academy played a big part in the Farhat children's education. The campus, located on Hammond Boulevard not far from their home on Normandy, has 150 acres of buildings and grounds offering grades K through 12. The Farhat children began to attend right after the start of the national school desegregation bussing program.

"I was going to Stillwell Middle School," said Cindy, "and my brothers were going to Normandy Elementary. Both weren't far from our new home on the west side. Stillwell was okay, I guess, and very diverse at the time. The next fall I was to attend Ed White High School, also close to Normandy Boulevard. That's when the whole bussing thing started."

Before they knew it, three of Cindy's brothers were going to be bussed right back to a school on the Northside—the place they left because of all the problems. That's when their lives abruptly changed again.

"On the first day of school," said Cindy, "my dad puts us all in the car and drops us all off at Trinity. We had no idea we were going to a private school. Luckily when I got there, a lot of my friends went there too because they were also about to be bussed. The situation was so bad, they were all sending their kids to Trinity. So it was a good transition."

Abie's son, 'Z,' went to Trinity for preschool, but not for elementary. Since they lived up on 103rd Street at the time, he attended Timaquana Elementary. When they moved to Orange Park, Z transferred to Trinity and stayed there until he graduated.

"Trinity has always had a good football team, but not back when my dad (Abie) went there. Now they recruit and have one of the bigger programs in the city, right up there with Bolles. Over all it was a good school though, with a dress code … meaning you had to wear a collar and slacks and all that."

Granddaughter Jamie was born in 1989 in Orange Park, so she also went to Trinity. By the time she enrolled, the teachers were well aware of the Farhat family. They already knew the parents, aunts, and uncles for quite some time.

Mom, Dad, and Grandma Sarah – mid 90s

"Every time I started a new class," said Jamie, "they'd say, 'Oh, another Farhat. Come on in.' I don't know if that meant for good or bad, because my uncles had more of a reputation when they were going to school there … they were party animals I guess. But I was smart and kind of quiet, and they were always surprised by it."

Transitions

Jamie recalls when she and her two brothers first went to their grandfather's house after Eddie's tragedy.

"It was scary, and very, very different. Not at all what we had expected. You know, when you're just a kid, a big change like that is definitely hard to adjust to. But they kind of treated us like royalty when we were little."

When something terrible happens to young people such as Jamie and her siblings, others in their age range might have a hard time understanding the true gravity of what occurred. At first the news strikes them as horrible, but after the initial shock, the friends tend to move on. Meanwhile, the victims have to deal with it for the rest of their lives. Sometime after moving in with their grandparents, their cousins accused Eddie's children of being spoiled. Such comments were likely confused with the result of loving care required for their situation. John and Jeanette treated their new children well, and always asked for their input on anything going on in their new family life. As for those comments by schoolmates or friends, they were outside of the situation and would never understand what it was like to lose both parents, particularly the way it happened. John and Jeanette listened, and then counseled them on how to respond.

Another factor contributing to the stress of their new life was their mother, who was still alive. Whether in jail during the trial for supervised visitations, or living free after the acquittal, she was still their mother and the expectation they would be with her at times was very great. It didn't matter if they believed she was innocent or not (which they do not believe). Knowing the confusion and pressure their grandchildren experienced, John and Jeanette were neither against nor for the mother being in contact. The fact they had that freedom seemed to help. They were always asked what they wanted to do, and they honored their answer. They never pushed them one way or the other.

Jamie noted that kind of freedom of choice extended to other areas of their lives. Whatever the situation, the children knew they could run it by their parents. When they did, John and Jeanette usually had an opinion, but in the end the children made their own choices.

Jamie was one of the Farhat offspring to go far with her education. While attending high school at Trinity, she took college courses at FCCJ—a dual enrollment program only the most motivated students can pull off. For Jamie, it was particularly forward thinking since she had no idea what she'd do with her studies: she only knew she should be in school (guidance from her grandfather no doubt). At first she thought she'd be a doctor, and took several pre-med courses. Still believing that was her direction, she enrolled at Florida State University to focus on biology—an essential foundation for medical school. However, half-way through FSU she realized she didn't want to go into the medical field at all. That could have been a problem since FSU wasn't cheap and Grandfather Farhat bankrolled her schooling.

According to Jamie, her grandfather had his heart set on her finding a career that made a lot of money. So when she changed her mind, she lost a lot of sleep over what he would think. When she finally told him she'd decided to study psychology instead of pre-med, he was surprisingly supportive. "Okay, whatever makes you happy." That was that. The relief Jamie felt could was indescribable. "I expected something completely different," she said, "like him being extremely angry or whatever. But he was supportive."

After she enrolled in NOVA Southeastern University's master's program in psychology, she decided to take yet another direction in life. She decided to get out of town for a while ... to Colorado.

Jamie would be the only one of her extended family to leave home—not just out of town or the state, but across the USA. She didn't say whether the reason stemmed from her father's death, but she did say she wanted to get away from her big family: an idea that both thrilled and overwhelmed her at times. Regardless, leaving home for a while fit right in with the rite of passage of millions of young Americans.

"I wanted a chance to branch out, to travel, and just to see who I am away from the whole family. It was kind of the best decision I ever made in all of my twenty-something years."

Since John left Ramallah for America in 1948, Jamie's break would be the first time any Farhat packed up and left town like that. The scary part for Jamie wasn't the travel so much as having to run yet another major change of plans by her grandfather. When she told him about med school, he was surprisingly amenable, but it helped that she planned to stay in town. What would he think when his granddaughter was about to spread her wings to fly west?

Because she was the only girl among the three siblings, Jamie spent the majority of her life in her grandparent's home. Added to that, Jamie and her grandpa had a very close connection which would make things harder. But she was determined the trip was something she had to do, and the hardest part was telling him.

It turned out to be another situation that was better than expected. When she finally sat down with John, he was naturally taken aback. But eventually he supported her. Maybe he saw in her the same intrepid spirit he felt when leaving Ramallah for America. Whatever the reason, he gave his blessing even if it took a while

"After I told him, it took six months for them to adjust to the fact." I was still at home so it seemed there wasn't a rush to let me know it was okay. But I was still going. By the time they saw my packed bags waiting at the door, they were more okay with it—not completely, but like, 'If you need money, let us know. We support you.'"

So she moved to Colorado and lived there for two years. First she lived in Longmont, and later moved to Boulder, closer to the Rocky Mountains. Although she was away from home, she continued her studies.

"When I gave up med school in FSU, I started grad school at NOVA. Then I switched to their online program and continued studies while I was in Colorado. I worked as a caregiver for the elderly when I was there and really enjoyed it. Because growing up with my grandparents and my great-grandmother before she passed, sort of gave me the experience of working with older people. I felt it was natural to take that kind of job. I wanted to help people, like I always do."

A year after returning to Jacksonville, she graduated with her master's degree from NOVA. Recently, she became a registered intern with the State of Florida serving with their mental health counseling team. Today, as the only daughter of Eddie Farhat Jr. she looks to her grandparents more as her parents, and has committed to help them through their waning years.

"Grandmother Farhat is a real character," she said, "and also the most honest person you're ever gonna meet. Like, genuine; if she has a feeling about something, she's going let you know about it. No-holds-barred. If something you're saying is upsetting her, you're going to hear about it. If you want an honest opinion, like if I have an outfit on and I need to know the truth about it, she will *talk* to me. She also has that generosity that my grandpa had too, sort of towards the whole family. She's always wanting people to come over and eat. She cooks all the time, and like everybody knows that's her favorite thing to do."

At St. John's Town Center – 2016

Baptism of Olivia – 2016

Chapter 16

Ma'a as-salaama

When Jamie left for Colorado, she had a feeling when she got back she would give full time care to grandfather, and maybe her grandmother as well. She told them before leaving that she'd only be gone two years and not to worry. She kept in close touch with John and Jeanette while she was away, and in late summer of 2015, she returned home. Her timing was good, because by then John's health had taken a real downturn. He was able to attend her graduation at NOVA's main campus in Fort Lauderdale, but that event would be one of the last outings he would make.

"The whole year I was back," said Jamie, "it was up and down like a roller coaster. Would he get better, or worse? It was hard to tell one week to the next because he kept going back and forth. Around the time we all thought he got better, the doctors sat us all down and told us he was in end-stage liver disease. They recommended we place him in Hospice, which was very hard for my grandmother to accept. She kept saying, 'Okay we'll take him home and we'll let things go from there.' But I told her 'No, grandma, this is more serious than that.' I tried to give her a reality check, but she wasn't really getting it."

The final month of John's life became a blur for the whole family. So much had happened, and there was real doubt as to whether he would make it. The situation was also perplexing because John only intended to go to the doctor about the intense pain in his knee—replaced several years earlier but with follow-up complications. The original appointment had been set, but the pain grew so intense that they admitted him to the emergency room. While there, the doctors decided he needed a knee operation right away. After the procedure, other complications emerged during what should have been his recovery period. Apparently, his malfunctioning liver set off negative dynamics in other parts of his body and everything started to shut down. But he was still mentally alert and able to talk with his family. To them, his mental acuity suggested he would be okay after all. But that was not to be.

John was hospitalized for the last time in October, 2016, at the age of eighty-three. A lot went wrong with John's body more or less all at once, starting with a bad infection that invaded his knee after the operation. Next, the infection got into his blood stream and assaulted his already ailing liver, which prevented the liver from functioning properly. He already had problems in that area, and the scar tissue that had built up prevented the liver from filtering and reproducing as it should. That in turn prevented the proper flow of blood, which inhibited the flow of nutrients, hormones, drugs, and naturally produced toxins. Essentially, most of John's organs began misfiring. His kidneys stopped working—initially caused by the anesthesia and compounded by his age. Events pushed him further down until his body couldn't keep up with the attack on his system. When things grew more serious, John's family kept a vigil in his hospital room.

One time after he suffered a severe setback, several members of the family were present and the doctors said they should talk about hospice again. As the discussion went on in his room, John's eyes were closed but he overheard the entire conversation among his children, spouses—everyone. Later that night when most of them had gone, John turned to Jeanette.

"What, did you all think I was going to die? Is that why everybody showed up at the same time?"

Of course she was surprised and couldn't say much, except that they were worried about him. Her confession seemed to give John strength, because the next day he was out of his bed and walking around the hospital. He made sure he got up from his bed under his own steam and went to the bathroom unassisted. Instead of returning to bed, he sat in the reclining chair next to the window. His candle burned brighter.

Father Al-Rahil visited John during the last few days of his life. He later recounted John's discussion about the Lord's Prayer, specifically the part that reads, "Forgive us our trespasses as we forgive those who trespass against us." John looked up at him and said, "So we have to forgive them, right Father?"

"That meant that whatever was on his mind," said Father Al-Rahil, "that scripture caused him to bring it up. John's wife and his sister were present during our conversation, and that was very significant because he must have forgiven whomever needed to be forgiven by him. He understood if there was anyone who needed forgiveness that he would do so. He was very close to meeting the Lord."

The question is whether John brought that up because of some unfinished work for the murderer of his son. But Father Al-Rahil said if that were true, it would have been only part of John's desire ... to be sure he'd forgiven *everybody* at that time.

"He got real good after that," Cindy recalled. "The day before they planned to send him home, we were there and mom had gone out to buy yogurt so she could feed him. While she was gone he got out of bed and sat in his chair having a good time cutting up with Buddy. Everything was great. My mom and dad had recently been at the Ritz Carlton Hotel for their anniversary. Each of our anniversaries were a week apart, and since we were together a lot, including traveling together, we celebrated our anniversary with them ... but not this time. Dad wasn't feeling so well, so they had to cut it short. The day he was supposed to go back home, Dad looked at me and said, 'Cindy, I'm not done yet. I'm going to take your mom back to that hotel so we can finish up that trip.' I said, 'You need to put her in the spa for the whole day and let them take care of her down there!' He always had plans. She was his whole world, and he was her whole world."

Since John displayed what looked like improved health, the doctors told him his family could take him home—not to Hospice, and not even to rehab, but home. They did, but apparently it was absolute hell as soon as he got inside the house. John said he didn't want a wheelchair. He didn't want to go back to a hospital bed. He didn't want a nurse, and he did not want to be transported again. "I want to sleep in our bed," he said to Jeanette. "I just want to be in my house with you."

In a short period of time, John was unable to walk or do much of anything. Less than twenty-four hours after arriving home, the family called the rescue services and he went right back to the emergency room. Then the family consulted with the doctors and among themselves about taking him to hospice. They decided it was time. Jeanette rode in the ambulance while the rest of the family followed in their cars. The whole time he was in the ambulance John kept asking for Buddy and Cindy. Jeanette told him they would be there when they arrived. Later as they rode through town, she said John kept looking out the window at the passing streets and houses … places he might never see again.

John was in hospice a little over three days, and throughout that time the entire family cycled in and out of his room. For the most part, Cindy was there as well as Jamie, Jeanette, and John's sister, Abla Bateh who also lives in Jacksonville. Cindy recalled their vigil by John's bedside as reminiscent of another time.

"It reminded me of something out of the New Testament, when someone was sick, like Lazarus. It was the women who stayed to watch over them. It's always the women, and that's how it was with my father. It seems like women can take it, but with my father, well, the men just kind of came and left. It was such a precious time to be there with him in his final hours."

According to the family, John's passing was so peaceful that no one even noticed. Not even the nurse. The staff came to check on him throughout the evening, and everything seemed fine. Then at around

4:00 a.m. another nurse came in and sat beside his bed to see if he was okay. He paused and looked closely at John. His expression was very peaceful, as if in a sound sleep. The nurse listened for his breathing, and then felt his heart and his pulse. Then he looked up and said, "He's stopped breathing."

Those who were there waited in silence until the rest of the family arrived. It took quite a while—a couple of hours—but during that time John's countenance remained vital, almost animated as if waiting for the rest of his beloved family to see him before his body followed his spirit. Cindy told her nephew, a funeral director who would prepare his body, not to alter her father's face in any way. She said when people behold him before he is buried, she wanted his fact to be exactly as it was that night.

A Very Green Thumb

Did my husband and I ever argue? Yes, of course! I can't tell you we didn't argue. It happened sometimes because of the kids. If they did something wrong he said, "They're your kids," and I told him, "No, they're your kids." Then by the time we go to sleep, everything is solved. We never have grudge after that. No, we never let the sun go down on our anger.

What can I say about him? He's such a good man. I wish he lived a bit longer. I didn't have any idea he was going to go that fast. But he was very sick for the last three or four years, and he suffered a lot. Some nights I didn't sleep maybe two minutes all night because I was with him. I didn't tell our kids in the store about him a lot because I didn't want to worry them.

But he loved his family. He told them to live right, not to lie, not to take advantage of anybody. Be straight all the time.

I used to tell him, I want a high-ceiling house, that I am tired of this house with the low ceilings. "Let's go," I said, "let's go." And he said, "If you want to kill me, move away from here." That was that. He didn't want to leave the kids and the properties.

He likes to plant, you know, and they used to sell vegetables, him and his mother, and I had to put up with it, but that was okay. All the people from our country came to buy the vegetables. Sometimes, you know, I'm not ready to have company, but when they buy vegetables John wants to bring them in for coffee. I said, "Oh boy," I used to get mad. I said when are we going to stop planting any vegetables? But they enjoyed it, so I put up with it no matter if I like it or not, I put up with it. I mean squash, the small squash, and people were dying to buy it. They used to come here from across town and buy it from my mother-in-law and my husband. They worked outside all the time and they had a great time. Things grew for them, but if I go up there, I make everything die.

My husband had a very green thumb that he got from his mother. She used to grow a garden in Ramallah all the time. One time when John was in the hospital and very sick, somebody brought him a flower that he could plant in the garden. I said, "When you go home, I'm gonna plant this flower

> and take care of it when you come home." And he said, "No, you gonna kill it. It's gonna die." But it died in the hospital. I didn't even bring it home.
>
> **Jeanette Farhat**

"His objective was to make sure all his kids were taken care of," said Buddy. "That was objective number one, and he was able to achieve that in his life. I know when he passed away, that he felt good that his wife and my wife—all the wives in his family—were definitely taken care of. That's the main thing. All Ramallah men tell their kids the same thing: 'Make sure mama's taken care of after I'm gone, and be sure she will never go hungry.' The kids are important for sure, but they're secondary. Mama, the wife, is the main one."

"That last night," recounted Jamie, "I went home and didn't really say anything. I always heard it said that before you leave you should say goodbye, or say something significant to them. But that night I was talking with someone and I just walked out without saying 'See you later,' or anything. After I got home I just kind of sat around waiting for the morning to go back to the hospital. But something told me I needed to go back *right now…* mostly because I felt like I should've said something before I left. So I went back very early in the morning, and when I got there I had a good talk with Grandfather. 'You know, Dad,' I said, 'I'm going to take care of Mom. Everything's fine, so you can rest if you want to go.' A couple of hours later, he passed."

"I was sitting in his room with my Mom," she continued, "when it happened. My grandma's sister—Samira, who came down from Michigan—slept on a little cot in the corner of the room, and my aunt Cindy had just left just to go sleep in the other room. Then he was gone. That was really, really tough."

"I remember one thing," said Cindy, "that will always, always be the sweetest memory of my life. It came after he had one particularly rough night in the hospital. It was October 6th, the night before Hurricane

Matthew struck, and he was already in the hospital for several days. Mom had gone home to take a shower and the rest of us were hanging out with Dad. He seemed to be doing okay, so I called mom and told her to just stay home a while. Sometime after the nurses helped him get to the bathroom, he said, 'Cindy, give me my nose glasses.' I said, 'What are you talking about, nose glasses?' I could tell all his senses were intact and he was talking a lot more. So the nurse smiled, 'He means oxygen … he's cutting up with you.'

"So I got the oxygen device and placed it around his nose. When I finished, he grabbed my hand and looked at me closely. 'I love you,' he said. I had this bad, sinking feeling he was telling me goodbye. I really struggled, and finally got up and walked out to the hallway because I couldn't stop crying. But I think he knew he wouldn't be around much longer, and he even tried to make me laugh with his funny nose glasses. But I think he knew at that point, and then I also knew. It was his time."

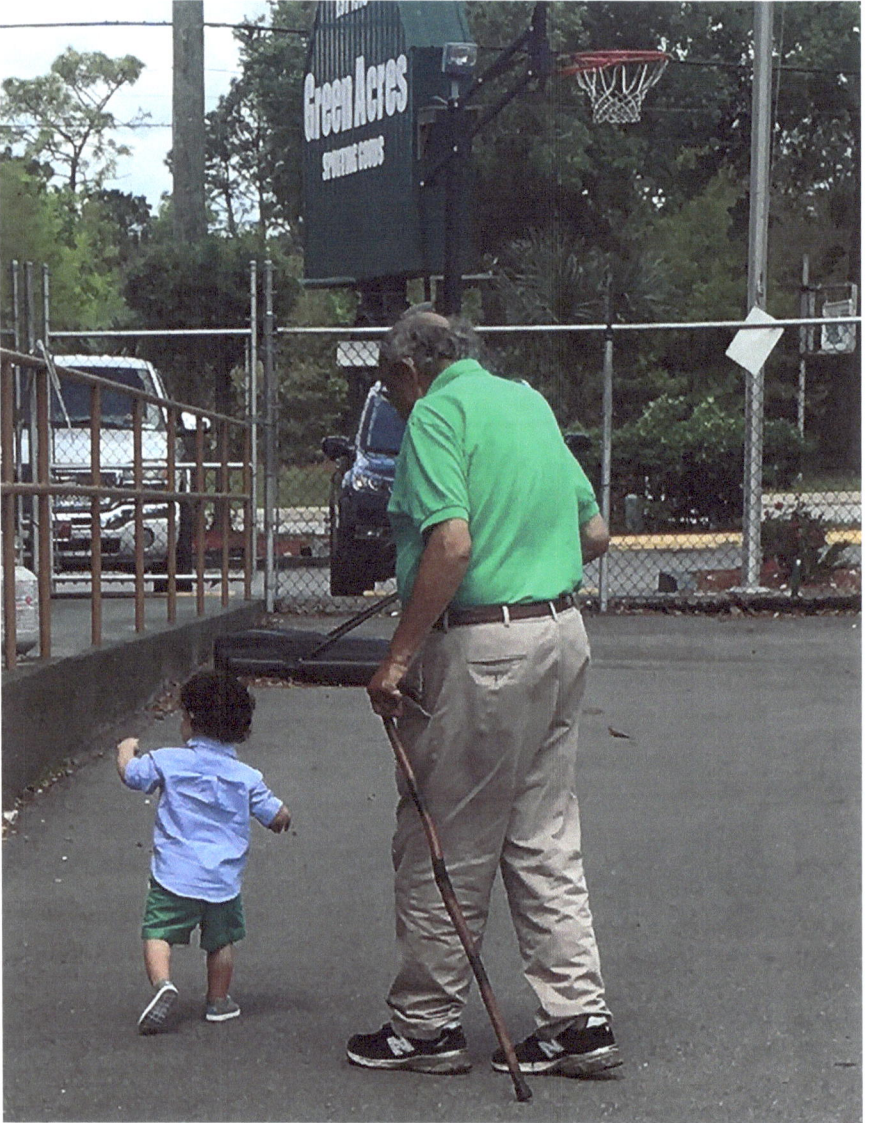

With baby Abie – 2016

www.ingramcontent.com/pod-product-compliance
Lightning Source LLC
Chambersburg PA
CBHW041957090426
42811CB00014B/1526